Thinking H

What should the primary history curriculum contain? How can history survive in an increasingly over-crowded and competitive school curriculum?

Thinking History 4–14 focuses on how to build on the National Curriculum by developing a creative, questioning approach to history. The author explores the practical tools with which the subject is taught, looks at the thinking behind history curricula and offers strategies to improve teaching and learning.

The book examines recent research on learning, teaching, curriculum and community within the National Curriculum. It provides teaching ideas for developing literacy, using questions, using visual and documentary sources and improving access to history. Practical advice on defining quality, assessment, local history, policy statements and curriculum planning are also included, alongside stimulating explorations of the nature of the discipline.

This book forms part of a series of key texts which focus on a range of topics related to primary education and schooling. Each book in the **Primary Directions Series** aims to review the past, analyse current issues, suggest coping strategies for practitioners and speculate on the future.

Grant Bage worked as a teacher and adviser before joining Cambridge University as a lecturer in education. He has led research and evaluation projects for English Heritage and the QCA and is particularly interested in curriculum leadership and in developing curricula through the use of story.

Primary Directions Series
Series Editors: Colin Conner, School of Education, University of Cambridge, and
Geoff Southworth, Department of Education Studies and Management, University of Reading

Assessment in Action in the Primary School
Edited by Colin Conner

Primary Education – At a Hinge of History?
Colin Richards

Science 3–13
The Past, the Present and Possible Futures
Edited by Paul Warwick and Rachel Sparks Linfield

Thinking History 4–14
Teaching, learning, curricula and communities
Grant Bage

Thinking History 4–14

Teaching, learning, curricula and communities

Grant Bage

ROUTLEDGE / FALMER

Taylor & Francis Group

London and New York

First published 2000
by RoutledgeFalmer
11 New Fetter Lane, London EC4P 4EE

Simultaneously published in the USA and Canada
by RoutledgeFalmer
29 West 35th Street, New York, NY 10001

Routledge is an imprint of the Taylor & Francis Group

© 2000 Grant Bage

Typeset in Times by
BOOK NOW Ltd
Printed and bound in Great Britain by
Biddles Ltd, Guildford and King's Lynn

British Library Cataloguing in Publication Data
A catalogue record for this book is available from the British Library

Library of Congress Cataloging-in-Publication Data
A catalog record for this book has been requested

ISBN 0-750-70873-5 (hbk)
ISBN 0-750-70872-7 (pbk)

For Teresa

Contents

Contents

Figures

Series Editors' Preface

In a context where the curriculum appears to be becoming increasingly narrowed by externally imposed initiatives, it is important to emphasise the benefits that are derived from retaining some breadth in the curriculum. This is effectively demonstrated by Grant Bage's contribution to the Primary Directions series, where he invites the reader to engage with some of the recurring issues of teaching and learning history with 4–14 year olds.

His thesis is that thinking is extended and expanded by enquiry into the challenging ideas that the study of history presents. He emphasises the importance of looking at history retrospectively as a precursor to projecting forwards to consider the place of history in childrens' educational future. He argues that it is difficult to imagine a society that has not learned from its past and that through consideration of the questions that are central to history we are contributing to the development of childrens' linguistic, cultural and technological understanding. As he suggests, 'we use what we learn not to pretend that the past, present and future are simplistically the same, but to examine how they are linked, how they differ and how we struggle to make sense from them all.'

The book contains a wealth of interesting and thought provoking evidence as well as stimulating examples that can be used to change practice in the classroom, all of which are 'grounded in the curriculum realities of the present'.

To borrow a further comment from the text, 'just like learning, history's main purpose is to prompt questions'. Each section opens with a variety of fundamental questions, addressed in the text that follows.

A final question asks, Can History survive? With the advice contained in this book there is no question that it can, and that it should. We are certain that every reader will gain something from this book and are delighted that Grant chose to include it in the Primary Directions Series.

Colin Conner and Geoff Southworth

Preface and Acknowledgements

This book was written as the Christian calendar edged from one millennium into the next. As clocks ticked through metronomic time so public interest in human time, in history, surged and swam. During the last decade, enormous numbers of people have been drawn to aspects and interpretations of the past. Interest in archaeology, museums, historical novels and films, family history and heritage tourism has perhaps never been so intense, nor so widespread.

Such contemporary enthusiasms are reflected in this book, but it also owes much to people who have spent a lifetime thinking about history and education. Some, such as John Fines, Bev Labbett or Alan Blyth, sadly died during the timespan of writing. Others continue with what, we may suddenly realise, turns out as a lifetime's work: to name Mike Corbishley, Christine Counsell, Peter Cunningham, Alan Farmer, Phil Gardner, Penelope Harnett, Roy Hughes, Bob Lister, Tim Lomas, Martin Oldfield, Ben Walsh and Andrew Wrenn is to cite but a few individuals, from whose views and ideas about history I have benefited during this book's gestation.

There are numerous others. The Historical Association and its Primary Committee fight a pretty good fight and with great conviviality. During various projects and initiatives it has been a stimulus and a pleasure to talk history or education with Andrea Christodoulou, Fiona Collins, Rob Grisdale, Amoafi Kwapong, Hugh Lupton, Andrew Lane, Patrick Redsell and Rachael Sutherland. During the last few years I have particularly enjoyed working with teachers and schools in Norfolk and Cambridgeshire on history courses; in Cambridgeshire with the 'Telling Tales' project; in King's Lynn and Greenwich through the story-telling initiatives of 'TASTE'; and in various odd locations with Suffolk Films. I have received practical assistance from Ken Bingham, Suzanne Fletcher, Christine Goad, Barbara Shannon and all the library staff at Cambridge University School of Education; and encouragement and help from Anna Clarkson and Rachel Larman at RoutledgeFalmer. I have been lucky enough to teach with gifted colleagues such as Colin Conner, Marion Dadds, Mary Jane Drummond and Martyn Rouse, and to learn in various courses alongside a great many talented and creative teachers. These people always leave me thinking, even when they did not mean to: this book owes them a great deal.

Finally, I would like to thank my family and friends, for putting up with yet another manuscript. You may not have written it, but you made it worth writing.

Grant Bage

Introduction: Mapping this Book

This is a signal to the world: we can transform vision into reality in the shortest possible space of time. Give us the bread and we'll give you the circuses. In twenty-eight months from depressed marshland to a Barnum and Bailey showground. 'And the vision is?' I asked. 'Er, time,' Mr. Gibbons replied. 'Time' he repeated, after a significant pause, remembering to capitalise the abstraction. I understood: millennium, zero longitude, Greenwich.

(Sinclair 1999 p. 30)

Mapping the Book

What is Education?

Schools rest upon resources such as books, computers and classrooms, resources which are deployed during events such as lessons, visits or meetings; yet education, especially high quality education, rests on far more than these. Education rests upon people: it takes them on social, spiritual and emotional journeys, as well as meeting practical and cognitive ends. Education prompts the uncertainties of change and questions, as well as the tangibles of 'targets hit' or 'skills developed'. During learning we balance the dream that education entails our improvement, against the threat that it confirms our stupidity. Education, in other words, rests upon the diversities of human agency and nature, as well as the predictabilities of systems of schooling.

This book tries to acknowledge such dimensions. It explores the practical tools and targets *with* which we conduct education, alongside the feelings and questions we conduct it *for*. It addresses practical problems of how to build on a particular example, such as the English 2000 national curriculum for history, alongside deeper questions of who, and what, history and education are 'for'. Its sister book (Bage 1999a) led with stories as a way into history: this sketches questions as a way into both.

History, as well as education, therefore pervades this text: as subject and object, as end and method. This book is a tiny piece of history itself since it is written and read, consciously developed from and constrained by, the specific 'times' of its context. To mirror such realities it has chronologic dimensions:

1

'retrospect' dominating Chapters 1 to 4, 'introspect' Chapters 5 to 8 and 'prospect' Chapter 9.

Drawing generally on others' writing, Chapters 1 to 4 review some important things we have come to know about history in education from the essentially retrospective stance of researchers. Insights from other researchers' and writers' work is represented in four chapters discussing learning, teaching, curriculum and community in history education. The next four chapters are located more 'introspectively', in recent and grounded practice. They offer examples of the author and other practitioners grappling with practical questions about history education, in the light of the year 2000 national curriculum in England for history. The themes of learning, teaching, curriculum and community match those of the first four chapters' but instead of a discursive exploration, each chapter offers a collection of policy or discussion papers. These address particular and often pressing needs by offering advice on, for example: teaching ideas and techniques for visual or documentary sources in history, techniques for differentiation in history, historical questions, overcoming the problems of historical language or defining best practice in local history. The final chapter also has practice in mind. Looking forward in 'prospect' it discusses questions which seem likely to grow in importance. The nine chapters of this book are grounded in the many classroom and curriculum realities of the present, but knitted together to help readers reflect upon theory alongside practice.

Since these discussions claim to be 'about history', specifically about 'history in education', they have pretensions to talk across time. Because studies of history suggest the ruinous nature of such an ambition, the pretensions are masked as underlying questions and issues. The authorial intention is nevertheless clear. This book attempts to define some perennial problems in history learning and teaching, across curricula and communities. That term 'perennial' typifies the intent. It means 'yearly' as in flowers or weeds but, as the Oxford English Dictionary has it, connotes eternity too: 'lasting through a long, indefinite, or infinite time'. As a teacher or learner of history, you may not have previously encountered every question or issue in this book: yet the claim is being made that if you pause to reflect you will recognise many in your past, present or possible future experience.

Such pretensions could slide to certainties and theoretical generalisation. My educational experience suggests that teaching, learning and leading are much messier in practice than generalised theories can cope with. If false certainties or dangerous over-generalisations are to be detected both writer and reader, you and I, must work hard together. For my part I can offer thoughts and experiences: the fruit of forty-three years of consciousness, of three degrees in history and education, of years of teaching, lecturing and research. To maximise openness I have organised these around questions and issues which pervade every chapter.

I can proffer these things but *we* will only profit if you do the same and reflect, as you read, upon what you already know. This book is therefore for testing, questioning and thinking. It is designed as a *thinking history* and needs you to think with it. Plunder ideas, borrow words, use reading to clarify where you disagree with the text. By the act of disagreement, come to know more clearly what you yourself think. Then teach a stronger lesson, learn a wiser history or write a better book. This title therefore embeds what 'authorities' tend to ignore: that a book only becomes educational through critical reading. This involves author and reader in comparing experiences and decisions. One of my first is to introduce this book, first published in the year 2000, by highlighting a metaphor, chosen from many which have laced its making (Taylor 1984).

That metaphor is ubiquitous: learning as journey (e.g. Ainscow, Hopkins, Southworth and West 1994 chapter 9, Conle 1997). Our journey refers to actual places in real time, visited through the English national curriculum in history. The metaphor therefore busies itself locating time and place, through lines on a map: latitude and longitude, as applied to learning and teaching about history. It starts in the place from where longitude is measured and Western scientific time begins: Greenwich, London, England.

This book comes from the England in which Greenwich is found. Greenwich the London village, Greenwich the Maritime Museum, Greenwich the domed icon of millennial Englishness. Greenwich, home since the seventeenth century to the Royal Observatory, home in the sixteenth century to Tudor monarchs, home to a million tourists' snapshots of England. Greenwich the multicultural London Borough, scene in 1993 of Stephen Lawrence's racist murder and a backdrop to his family's struggle for English justice. Greenwich, a Local Education Authority desperate to improve levels of school and family literacy. Greenwich, where the TASTE project has worked to promote teaching-as-storytelling and connect local with global (e.g. Bage 2000a, 2000b; Collins 1999 and 2000). Greenwich, home to the once-disputed 'Greenwich Meridian' now linking half our world. The North Pole, the South Pole, hot seas and cold seas, Britain and Ghana, France and Togo, Spain and Burkina Faso, Algeria and Mali: places cleaved to 'Greenwich' time despite different histories, peoples and environments.

Longitude is therefore this book's leading metaphor, as measured through the Greenwich meridian. Longitude 'the tool', a certainty craved by sailors to mark their place at sea. Longitude 'the imaginary line' that helped them to do so. Longitude the contemporary 'educational link', seizing 'the opportunity of the new millennium to focus our attention on the future of our planet and on our role as global citizens' (Oxfam 1999). Then there is longitude 'the massively successful book' epitomising a contemporary international thirst for interesting stories from history (Sobel 1995). 'Longitude the quest' was pursued, if Sobel is correct, by many a crank, academic and astronomer royal: but attained through craft and practice by John Harrison, humbly educated carpenter turned clockmaker, obsessive and perfectionist practitioner. Harrison's 'simple' discovery took a lifetime to develop: he made clocks that measured time at sea. Comparing time measured by these clocks against time measured by the sun showed up a difference and from that difference longitude was measured. When intersected by the easily defined 'latitude', an exact position became clear.

Like all metaphors 'longitude' has limits. This book will not sell as many copies as Sobel's, nor narrate an heroic story like Harrison's, nor provide the mathematical certainties of atomically measured time: it cannot tell educators exactly what to do or where to be. What it can sketch is a map, drawn from the author's experience in teaching, learning and researching history with 4 to 14 year olds. Upon this map lines of thinking are traced; with this map we may journey, educationally, through this book's nine chapters and beyond.

The map offers four lines of educational longitude, visible in industrialised and many past European societies. These lines represent *learning* and *teaching* about history; the history *curriculum* as in deciding what to teach; and how *communities* place history in context. Intersecting these four longitudes are latitudinal lines embodying political control, cultural diversity, media, values, democracy, cognition and social context. Where these lines of educational longitude and latitude cross on our map, an underlying question is asked. These questions are referred to in every chapter apart from the last, when new ones are raised.

These questions ask you as reader to consider extremes and in so doing, to choose your own direction. They are offered as a navigational aid for educational journeys through history. Elucidating such choices pervades the author's own practice (e.g. Bage 1993; Bage 1999a), have been described elsewhere in history education (e.g. Claire 1996; Fines and Nichol 1997; Husbands 1996; Lee 1984, 1991; Turner-Bisset 1999) and are grounded in broader scholarship exploring educational choices and dilemmas, especially for teachers (e.g. Alexander 1995; Berlak and Berlak 1981; Gardner 1993; Hargreaves 1994; Hoyle and John 1995; Stenhouse 1975; Van Manen 1991). This map adapts some of that work to widen the view for history educators. Nevertheless, on an everyday basis teaching and learning are practical and personal activities, experienced locally and often instantaneously. Practitioners tend to tack between extremes, tempering such educational generalisations as crystallised in our 'underlying questions' with pragmatic and flexible decision making. Everyday, practical educational success does not rest in 'reaching' longitudinal or latitudinal polarities; but in using them to locate where in the world we are, as teachers and learners, and where we could travel to next.

Mapping a 'Thinking History': Questions and Issues

The grid opposite is a navigational aid for educational journeys through history. Important issues define its longitude and latitude. The 'underlying question' in each box encapsulates a choice between opposing directions. In practice the daily, local journeys of teaching and learning involve pragmatism, necessitating practitioners to tack between such axes. Equally, skilled teachers possess a clear sense of their own and their children's overall destination and set clear, long-term learning courses. Not all important questions or issues can be included and as reader you can devise your own; those below are merely common enough in practice or scholarship to steer this book.

This particular journey starts figuratively from Greenwich for the educational, social, cultural and historical reasons previously stated. Howerever young and

	Issues about how history			
	Learning	**Teaching**	**Curricula**	**Communities**
Governance issues	Is pursued for instrinsic or extrinsic ends.	Adheres to predicted plans and objectives or responds to children's needs.	Are locally or nationally defined.	View schools or central government as key controllers of the curriculum.
Issues of diversity	Starts from the curriculum's requirements or different children's needs.	Interacts with the whole child or only the student.	Are inter-disciplinary or subject specific.	Promote singular or multicultural histories in schools.
Media issues	Is only communicated through writing or is expressed via other media.	Standardises or differentiates pedagogy and materials.	Advance multimedia or only written literacy skills.	Interact with their history through popular as well as specialist media.
Values-led issues	Develops multiple or singular intelligences.	Is perceived as technical delivery or moral art.	Open adults' values to scrutiny or promotes their acceptance.	Are comprehensive or selective in their aspirations for history.
Democratic issues	Increases or decreases a child's dependence on the teacher.	Challenges or implements a school's stated aims for learning history.	Reveal or obscure the grounds for history's claims to value.	Are active or passive in pursuit of their own histories.
Cognitive issues	Aims for knowledge through questioning or memorisation.	Promotes transmission or analysis of historical knowledge.	View history as a social activity or one pursued only in school.	Understand history as school work or lifelong knowledge.
Social issues	Is designed for groups or individuals.	Emphasises personal interpretation or social control.	Are negotiated teacher to child or standardised.	Perceive historical knowledge as made individually or collectively.

global the author would like to think himself, in reality he is a white, middle-aged Englishman: the world sketched is seen through his eyes. For *he,* well *he* must now come clean and admit it is *I,* is not saying where *you* should be, or go. Rather I am trying to show you places which I have visited, enjoyed, wish never to see again or may yet end up. Our journey and this book therefore begins by visiting the first and most important longitudes of education: learning.

Section 1
Retrospect

1   Learning History

I was transfixed by the way time buckled, met itself in pleats and folds; I stared at a picture in a book of a safety pin from the Bronze Age – a simple design that hadn't changed in thousands of years . . . I stared at pictures of prehistoric bowls, spoons, combs. To go back a year or two was impossible, absurd. To go back millennia – ah! that was . . . nothing.

(Michaels 1996 p. 30)

Mapping the Questions

Underlying Questions About How History Learning:

Is pursued for instrinsic or extrinsic ends	*Governance Issues*
Starts from the curriculum's requirements or different children's needs	*Issues of Diversity*
Is only communicated through writing or is expressed via other media	*Media Issues*
Develops multiple or singular intelligences	*Values-led Issues*
Increases or decreases a child's dependence on the teacher	*Democratic Issues*
Aims for knowledge through questioning or memorisation	*Cognitive Issues*
Is designed for groups or individuals	*Social Issues*

Just like history, one of *learning's* main purposes is to prompt questions. As a critical reader you bring your own to this text. As its writer I shall explore some which have underlain my own classroom practice, curriculum development and research experience over the last couple of decades. These are highlighted in the map sketched in the introduction. They preface each of these first four chapters, they help locate the policy and practice of Chapters 5 to 8 and they will be discussed again during the final chapter. A brief overview now will set these opening chapters in context and perhaps stimulate you as reader to reflect further upon your own learning opinions, experiences and questions.

Fundamental to much educational thinking, especially from the time of Rousseau, has been the question of whether children learn about a subject such as history because it is intrinsically interesting and useful; or for extrinsic reasons such as promoting 'citizenship' or 'national identity'. Although such a question may appear as remote from practice as a superceded national curriculum, skilful teaching translates or embodies such structures into learning that feels friendly and intrinsic to students (see Bage 1999a). Many everyday pedagogic skills lie in navigating children's learning through such choppy curricular waters: or, on carefully considered occasions, refusing to take to sea at all. History is in particular need of such sympathetic and assertive treatment, being centrally concerned with the fragments of the past still present in our children's 'here and now'.

This leads to a related question. Does learning start from the curriculum's requirements or different children's needs? To an extent, before the advent of national curricula such a question about educational history could be sidestepped. Within living memory, in primary schools teachers could ignore history as a subject or mould it to fit 'their' children's perceived individualities: differences in age, ethnicity, geography or social class, for instance. Such independence is perhaps atypical. In the overall history of formal history curricula, teachers' autonomy has more often been circumscribed. Throughout the twentieth century secondary history students have followed largely pre-ordained exam courses and syllabi, shaped more by traditional structures than learners' needs, or the worlds beyond school. Related criticisms could be made of elementary, textbook-led history courses in Victorian England (e.g. Gosden 1969 pp. 31, 38) or today's subject-led national curricula.

Some classic ways in which history teachers have attempted to translate such curricula into learning are suggested by the next questions on our map. These ask whether history learning should be communicated only through writing, or whether it should rely upon 'varied media' and developing 'diverse intelligences'. This book argues towards the latter in both cases, not from sentiment but for efficiency and effectiveness. Subjects which fail to relate to other subjects produce a narrow range of learning, and face an increasingly perilous curricular future; especially in societies where information is as widespread, and work skills as fluid, as in the industrialised Northern world.

The fifth and sixth questions on our map about learning tap similar fundamentals. Do the ways in which we organise our history classrooms 'decrease or increase a child's dependence on the teacher?' In parallel, do history curricula 'aim for knowledge through questioning or memorisation?' It seems a consensual assumption that the coming world will require people to be increasingly confident learners, able to question more than memorise masses of information for their work (e.g. Askew and Carnell 1998; Beare and Slaughter 1993; Day 1999). Such an aspiration contrasts with most state-sanctioned nineteenth century curricula, when textbook or exam history typically promoted rote and decontextualised memorisation, at least for the masses. This typical critique of prevailing primary history was made in 1867:

> No attempt is made to interest the pupil in his studies by teaching him the broad principles or general applications of the various branches of knowledge . . . proficiency is sought to be attained by cramming the pupils to bursting-point with definitions, dates, and figures . . . wholly uninteresting and practically useless to students . . .
>
> (quoted in Gosden 1969 p. 31)

Before we become too complacently modernist, within forty years much had changed. Edwardian history educators were claiming that the acquisition of logic and the development of thoughtful citizenship, formerly an expectation of adult elites, could be learnt by all adolescents through studying history (e.g. Bridge 1907; Fletcher 1907; Howard 1905). The foundations for such curriculum development could and were being laid in at least some primary schools. Although 'learning logic and citizenship through history' might appear remote to young children, some Edwardians argued that it could be achieved:

> The child's interest must be won . . . by . . . an incident and event that arouses him, as we can see quite clearly in his games, where he loves to be acting . . . however the ultimate aim need not be forgotten. We can teach a child to reason, even when we are telling him a story.
>
> (Neild 1907 pp. 290–1)

Recent national curricula may have been the first to legislate for cross-phase history learning in England, but its desirability had long been argued.

Finally, in this introduction. Should history learning 'be designed for groups or individuals?' As with most of the issues traced on our map, a characteristic of effective history teachers is that they seem able to plot courses between such polarities. A fine teacher can retain the wholeness of a class, simultaneous with stimulating personal learning. A fine teacher balances creating memories with questions; and offers a child independence, simultaneous with maintaining contact. In fine teaching, group events leave beneficial marks on individual minds: marks which we call learning. Often a fine teacher may be unaware that she has done so at the time, and a learner unaware of her impact until much later in life. This young, contemporary teacher remembered her history learning from some twenty years previously:

> As a child I remember hearing the story of the Fire of London. I was sat on the carpet in my classroom, surrounded by open-mouthed six year olds, and the storyteller was Mrs Harwood. She told it well and we were there among the flames and the screaming crowds. I could smell the smoke, feel the terror . . . I knew this really happened and I knew it happened a 'long time ago', but I couldn't have told you when or given you any more factual information. Instead I was given images and impressions that are still with me today. I'm sure Mrs Harwood did supply us with facts and figures it's just that they 'evaporated' . . . dry facts left me cold and I could never remember them anyway – I failed my GCSE history . . .
>
> (Froggatt 1998 p. 1)

In broader social terms memory is a:

> Key mediating term between the individual and society . . . Our intentions for the future are grounded in the past and without remembering we cannot see, for how else would we know what we see?
>
> (Tonkin 1992 pp. 98, 104)

In educational terms, learning history is something of a social equivalent to personal memory. We shall now therefore move on from underlying learning questions in our map of thinking history, to more immediate aspects. These start with learning about time and memory, before moving on to consider historical knowledge and understanding, historical interpretations, historical enquiry, organisation and communication. These categories mirror 'historical know-ledge, skills and understanding' as presented in the year 2000 English national curriculum in history (DfEE 1999a).

Time and Memory

Language and memory define humanity: by lending access to past and present experience, they help humans construct visions of a future towards which we work. Memory and language are also interdependent. Memory needs language to name its memories, but language needs memory if users are to become skilful in language's turns and terms. Learning rests upon the increasing degrees of intellectual precision which a child's developing memory provides, memory then being employed to interpret feelings, objects, people and symbols. Learning anything involves remembering things about it: and often, though not always, remembering more about it. If people need such memories, so do societies. Laws, customs, cultures and technologies rest upon memory. Although the centrality of memory to individual and societal learning broadly buttresses history's educational status, learning history involves more than 'remembering'. History in schools entails asking and answering questions about the past, making selections from memories or records, and joining these selections together into an explanatory narrative (Bage 1999a). Interpretation of memories becomes the distinctively educational ingredient.

There are also many ways of remembering and interpreting other than those offered by history. Literature, art, science, indeed most intellectual disciplines, remember and interpret experience. Hence for instance 'natural history's' foundation in the story of science, or the importance of 'the autobiographical' in literature and art. These reasons alone lend history learning a powerful and broad curricular function, but the construction of memory in individuals mirrors learning about history in another important way. Like an individual's memory, learnt history is a social construct, built from interactions between individual preferences and experiences and those of the people, power groups and struc-tures within which our lives are embedded:

> Infants initiate: they do not just respond or copy. But they can only become human through interaction with other persons and the whole environment . . . cognition, the ability to think, is developed interactively. The world outside is used to build the means of understanding that same outside world, and as we grow, we continue to process and internalise the outside to think with, as well as to think about . . .

> (Tonkin 1992 pp. 105, 104)

This anthropological and psychological argument leads to the conclusion that we need to learn history not just because history is one of society's most important ways of remembering and learning about itself; but because our very own, personal memories also derive from without, as much as within (Morton 1993). When we learn about 'the past' in general we are not just extending knowledge and experience of others. We are also learning how to think about our own past, present and future, faculties essential to expanding children's minds (e.g. Crites 1986).

A growing understanding of time generally develops naturally, as children's memories and experiences widen. Donaldson (1978) discovered that socially contextualised tasks helped young children show more abstract thinking than had previously been discerned. In parallel a recent researcher concluded that in the context of discussing literary and historical stories 'Children between the ages of three and seven evidently try to use the terminology of time measurement' and have 'a grasp of the key historical concepts of change and continuity. They know what has gone for good. They also know that other things still exist' (Hoodless 1996 pp. 108, 109). Talking with peers and adults seemed crucial to younger children learning about time: 'the major implication . . . is the need for teachers to listen to children talking rather than constantly talking to them' (ibid. p. 116). Lee (1991) and Edwards (1978) have drawn similar conclusions concerning the secondary curriculum. Effective learning about time and history entails constructing curricula and classrooms in which extended, challenging talk is possible: rich in historical dialogues between learner and teacher, learner and learner, and learners and 'texts' of multiple types. Out of such dialogues a whole range of knowledge grows, starting with language and memory, extending to time and then using a combination of the three as the foundation for 'history'.

Historical Knowledge and Understanding

The 2000 English national curriculum in history asks that children learn about the characteristics and diversity of past societies, some reasons for and results of historical change and how to link their expanding knowledge into an overview of history. This seems reasonable, but how does it relate to theories of learning and learning history?

Empirical studies of 7 to 14 year old children learning history in school suggested some identifiable, relatively common and hierarchical levels of learners' understanding of history, at least when children responded to 'history' presented in conventional, textbook, test-related, and paper-based style (Lee, Ashby and Dickinson 1996). Their six levels contrasted less effective models of understanding such as historical evidence 'being presented as unproblematic information', with more effective models such as 'historical evidence needs viewing in its historical context'. Progression in historical learning as constructed through such levels may not be 'tied directly to age' (ibid. p. 74) but this research held out the hope that a detailed model of progression could be developed to influence educational practice and policy.

This hope has not yet materialised and the ever-more-general nature of the assessment tools offered within national curriculum history (e.g. Bage 1993; Phillips 1998) illustrate a practical reality. We cannot at present assemble sufficiently reliable, hierarchical pictures of how younger children learn or know history from which to generalise, either at theoretical or policy levels. This does not mean that classroom practitioners do not already 'know' lots about learning in history, derived from experience and values. Indeed practitioners may know more than theorists, even though they rarely gain the chance to explicate it. Lee, Ashby and Dickinson's (1996) project was influenced by previous research modelling older students' history learning: it did not derive from looking afresh at how 5, 7 or 9 year old children appeared to be learning history. Problems with developing overarching theories of historical learning may also have arisen because their research could not develop from a sufficiently wide range of everyday classroom settings and practices, over a long enough period of time. Or, it could be that the nature of historical thinking will never be totally accessible to observation, especially in younger children.

It does not follow from this that 'theories about learning' are irrelevant to history. For instance Gardner's theories, although contested, have much to say about learning, schools and history. He identified a range of seven intelligences which education could develop, alongside three stages through which formal school systems expected most learners to progress (Gardner 1993). The seven intelligences were the linguistic, interpersonal and intrapersonal, to which history as a traditional school subject is closely related; and the logical-mathematical, spatial, musical and bodily-kinesthetic, from which school history is perhaps more distant. The three stages of learning are the intuitive, the scholastic and the disciplinarian, although Gardner claims that the first and third types of learning manifest at any age, not hierarchically as schooling envisages. Indeed he identifies many educational problems arising because of disjunctions between these stages. For instance the intuitive younger learner of 9 years old, using observation of a local building to guess at its history, may shortly be pitched by secondary transfer into abstracted or textbook-style evidence and questions concerning historical causation of a distant event. These, although conforming to what traditional views may expect of a scholastic, schooled 11 year old, may bear little relation to experience and can leave children floundering. One theoretical and long-argued for solution (e.g. Stenhouse 1975) is to emphasise how learners should work towards the characteristics of the third stage, the discipline, as their objectives. In some ways this is what a national curriculum in history can 'do' (e.g. Cooper 1995b) and do well. It can offer teachers, especially non-specialist historians, a clearer picture of the learning that 'thinking history' entails. In practice many pitfalls lie in the way. Political influences over the curriculum often outweigh educational ones. For instance children's notional coverage of national history may be considered more politically important than gaining an in-depth understanding of, say, historical change at a smaller scale. The curriculum is skewed accordingly (e.g. Phillips 1998) and children's learning suffers (Lee 1991). Conservative influences extant in school organisation, architecture and culture (Alexander 1995; Galton 1995) also colour the ways in which teachers view children's learning, and are filters through which the learning objectives of disciplines are viewed. For instance, a sample of nearly thirty primary history teachers interviewed in a recent research project were reluctant publicly to admit to 'not teaching' aspects of history identified by a national curriculum. It was also obvious from their responses, from their children's learning and from concurrent government attempts to slim the curriculum, that the breadth of stipulated content was unrealistic for teachers to cover at KS2 (Bage, Grisdale and Lister 1999). The combined weight of public expectation, political pressure and professional pride seemed to conspire against these teachers exercising discretion to 'leave out' history curriculum content. From an opposite perspective, a study of a secondary school's history department's attempts to organise a term's learning for 13 year olds around Gardner's theory of multiple intelligences also revealed structural influences on history learning. Students and teachers overall responded well to the initiative. They valued the variety a consideration of 'multiple intelligence' encouraged in teaching styles, and the opportunities it offered for students to articulate and evaluate different areas of learning. The study also identified that testing of theory could not easily be disentangled from testing of the social contexts in which the theory was initiated. Patchy teacher knowledge, conservative parental and student expectations, the problems of cross-curricular planning in subject-centred secondary schools and the habitual expectations of students to be told to write and to pursue closed tasks: these 'problems' appeared to inhibit the theory as much as obvious faults within the theory itself (Chong 1997). As individuals we know also how crucial emotions are to learning (e.g. Askew and Carnell 1998), aiding us at times of confidence and strength, slowing us at points of stress or fragility. In other words it is difficult to see how any theory of children's knowledge about history, whether it comes from a researcher, teacher or government policy, can simply be 'read off' from an abstract record and applied unproblematically to practice. When children learn history in school they learn what school tells them, as well as what history tells them. Models of children's learning in history that ignore the importance of teachers' learning, or institutional inertia, or children's feelings, or other influences such as family, social and media-led learning, are unlikely to be effective in school contexts.

Such everyday influences upon learning rarely appear at policy level, where different contexts produce different pressures to which policymakers respond. The learning models that dominate educational politicking are governed more by the generalisations of daily newspaper headlines, yearly budgets or the short cycles of electoral logic and public opinion; less by the particular needs suggested by a child's twelve years of compulsory schooling, or a teacher's forty year career. Yet on an everyday basis, as teachers we ground our approaches to learning in local soil: enriched perhaps by grand theory and national policy, but improving practice by observation, experience and our own immediate actions (e.g. Brookfield 1995).

Learning history is about learning how to view the past through as many such lenses as possible; refining how to apply Gardner's multiple intelligences, for instance, as much as it is 'knowing more' about the Industrial Revolution or

Ancient Greece. Learning about learning history follows a similar process. There is guidance on how to achieve this in our introductory map, in many wise models summarised in Chapter 2, in many concrete examples of practice and policy in Chapters 5 to 8, and in many of the demands of the English national curriculum in history. Having said that, because it is still up to us to learn it and apply it, individualisation is essential. As a well-grounded recent research study of teacher-knowledge in history concluded:

> . . . teaching is a deeply complex, intellectual and practical activity. It is a creative act in which the expert teacher selects from the store of experience and repertoire of her teaching strategies and representations, the most appropriate ones for her or his purposes. The danger in focusing only on teaching skills and competences or standards . . . is that it ignores the complex reasoning, thinking and synthesis which underpins the best teaching.
>
> (Turner-Bisset 1999 p. 52)

Historical Interpretations

Experiencing stories, especially traditional stories, lays foundations for young children's understanding of time, events and people (e.g. Applebee 1978; Bage 1999a; Cooper 1995a); but history is more than folk tales. Historians' stories purport to be real and testable, to derive from evidence, to explain how and why actual events happened or failed. At the heart of this process is the building and comparing of stories: interpretative, explanatory stories that may resemble the stories of literature, but which are required to pass different tests. Cooper (1995a) has brilliantly described how young children can begin learning this historical process from the ages of 2 and 3, through 'everyday' activities such as play, television or story. She also shows how, on their own, these are insufficient for learning history. Teachers and schools have crucially important roles to play in sensitively linking the natural imaginative activities of children, such as make-believe about the past, to the more formal and structured mental activities of 'history'.

In many ways this describes what history teachers 'do' for learners between the ages of 4 and 14. We induct them into some principles of history and motivate learners to think like historians. On its own this is a major task but since the introduction of the national curriculum teachers have felt under other, intense and conflicting pressures, many reflected in our educational map. The varied needs of children, the demands of a centrally imposed and not necessarily child-friendly curriculum, the disciplines of the subject and the many practical difficulties of teaching in modern times can make the support of history learning a daunting task. Fortunately, understanding 'historical interpretations' is at least one aspect of history education in which such pressures pull in the same direction. The 2000 English national curriculum in history enshrines 'interpretations' (DfEE 1999a), aided and abetted by the introduction of 'citizenship' and by learning objectives promoting critical reading in the primary English national literacy framework (DfEE 1998) and secondary national curriculum English (DfEE 1999c).

In practice, learning about 'historical interpretations' therefore involves sophisticated, inter-disciplinary curriculum planning and more than just considering opposing viewpoints of this or that historical event. It entails developing some specific and fundamental approaches to learning, expounded by Bruner:

> The first of these is the idea of *agency:* taking more control of your own mental activity. The second is *reflection:* not simply 'learning it in the raw' but making what you learn make sense, understanding it. The third is *collaboration:* sharing the resources of the mix of human beings involved in teaching and learning. Mind is inside the head, but it is also with others. And the fourth is *culture,* the way of life and thought that we construct, negotiate, institutionalize and finally (after it's all settled) end up calling 'reality' to comfort ourselves.
>
> (Bruner 1996 p. 87)

Such approaches were illustrated in some Y3 children's historical learning with which I was recently involved, through the Cambridge Nuffield History Project. The children's class teacher, Patricia Aves, recorded, analysed and wrote up her reflections upon a series of lessons in which 7 and 8 year olds learnt about Ancient Egypt. The school is a state school serving a socially mixed catchment area.

What Patricia described does focus upon 'historical interpretations' in the sense of the 2000 English national curriculum history (DfEE 1999a). It also extends beyond that specific into Bruner's broader educational tools of agency, reflection, collaboration and culture, in the learning of the teacher as well as the children. I therefore quote from it at some length and include an extract from a child's writing at the end:

> The aim of the fifth lesson was not only to enjoy a story and try to set it in context, but also to challenge the children to consider the often perplexing nature of history when evidence is not clear or interpretations are debatable. It involved Queen Hatshepsut . . . The story as told here (Macdonald and Starkey 1996) has many layers which can be explored . . . it stimulated much discussion . . . I then gave the children a translation of a short text discovered on the wall of the temple of Queen Hatshepsut . . . This was compared to the story we had already heard . . . The children were asked to think why there were differing versions of the story, why the story of the God blessing Hatshepsut was on the wall of her temple and why her statues were broken or changed and her name and images scratched out.
>
> What was interesting was that no-one said that the story on the wall could not be true because a god could not really send such messages . . . We had entered the realm of fairy stories . . . The children were at a stage where the merging of fact and fiction is acceptable. No-one questioned the story of the god, though they agreed that Hatshepsut would have had the story carved on the wall so that the people believed that she should be the queen. Rightly or wrongly I did not push them to think further . . . Some children set about

writing a structured report drawn from the wall painting . . . I asked others to try to write their answers to some of the questions raised by the story of Queen Hatshepsut. The way they tackled those answers made me see that they were developing critical and logical thinking and that the best way of aiding this development was to give them opportunities to use their powers of reasoning and imagination . . . None of the children had found the work easy but all had contributed to the discussion and some had really pushed their thoughts into new areas. Mica for instance:

Mica   31 March 1998   Queen Hatsheput

The story that she wrote on the wall said that Queen Hatsheput wanted everyone to know that women have a rite to be pharohe. I think she wrote it because she wanted to be pharohe. The next story says that Hatsheput would not come off the throne she stayed on and got herself crowned. I belive the second storoy was true because the rule was no women were allowed to be pharohe. They belived that only a man could lead the army. I belive men are very strong but some women are strong to.

To be a good rule you need tallent, strenth and bravery. Good aiming with weapons and protection. Kindness sometimes crulness and not to be frightend of other people. You need a good thinking brain. This could be anyone man or woman.

(Aves 1998 pp. 15–16)

Historical Enquiry

A major problem with analysing learning is that atomising it into parts or aspects misrepresents their mutual nature, as Mica's far-ranging discussion above shows. The national curriculum summarises historical learning using the five usefully simple elements heading the sections of this chapter. It can also over-emphasise their separateness. Asking questions is an interpretative act depending upon which aspects of knowledge are being pursued, in what timescale, and for what purpose. 'Historical evidence' is not an end in itself, but a means to pursuing an enquiry or answering a question. This is why national curriculum history's listing of the different sources of evidence that children should use, such as pictures, music or buildings, lies adjaceant to its requirement that students ask and answer historical questions.

Such an emphasis upon learning processes led Gardner to an interesting argument, of direct relevance to history learning. His contestable observation that many schools failed to motivate children's interest, whilst most museums did (Gardner 1993 pp. 201–2), speaks directly to the necessity for schools to vary learning styles in history. The materials and tasks for historical learning need to be varied, children need to learn as do apprentices through observation, and the learning of children beyond school needs to be reinforced through practical, stronger home–school links. Practical, local enquiries provide a context for such things: and if none are to hand then the subject matter of history needs to be made practical and local through appropriate teaching styles, as happened with Mica above.

Questions fuel history, which is why you will find scores of examples to test out in Chapter 5. Teachers' questions are important, but only insofar as they act as models and prompts for those in which children have a genuine stake and over which they have some control. The Nuffield History Project came to understand this, drawing from close observations of children learning history and its participants' teaching practices to argue that:

> The pupils' asking of questions at the start of a history-led project can serve many useful functions. It provides the children with a personal view and a constant point to which later study can be referred. It provides the teacher with a wealth of material if, as is the intention, the questions are used as the basis for project content. Quite simply, the children ask the questions and together teacher and pupils begin to answer them.
>
> (Fines and Nichol 1997 p. 56)

Such a model emphasises the importance of social, personal and emotional aspects of learning referred to earlier. Equally it does not abandon a traditional pedagogic role, namely to lead children into new ways of thinking which, without schools, they may not discover. This experienced teacher considered herself a 'non-historian' but used Nuffield principles to extend her historical questions and reflect upon her own practice, during a local history project with Y2 children. I quote her at some length simply to encourage us as readers to attempt the same.

> I think in previous years, I have given the children 'answers' too easily, for example when they appeared not to know. This project has developed my confidence . . . By altering my questioning to become open-ended I now can allow for the many different answers that children give and no one answer is 'right'. When the children see that their every try is receiving praise . . . it encourages the more reticent child . . . By using speculative questions, I feel the children are more at ease and can form a theory . . . This I believe encouraged them to have the confidence to debate issues independently, use questions, to persist and chat in their pairs or groups without the teacher always in control . . . It was interesting for me too to stand back, observe and listen.
>
> (Mann 1997 p. 19)

The Nuffield History Project also drew upon Bruner to emphasise that historical learning benefits from being expressed in varied forms. These form a holy trinity of knowledge and learning or, if you prefer, a magic triangle. They are *enactive learning* in which play, drama, role play and physical participation through arts and crafts are emphasised; *iconic learning*, from visual representations; and *symbolic learning* from forms of language. Most people reading this will have experienced these types of learning, and probably emphasised the former over the latter as they grew older. This in itself can be an error. No theory of learning supports the view that 14 year olds are too old to learn history through drama or pictures, or that 5 year olds are too young to learn through language, such as story. Fine teachers instinctively use a mix of resources to support historical learning in these different forms. Unfortunately, students' performance in most public examinations in history is still assessed more by written answers to somebody else's historical questions, less by assessing how students ask and answer their own questions, using a range of media. Until this basic fact alters insights into broader aspects of learning such as Bruner's, however well grounded, can make only limited impact upon practice.

Organising and Communicating

It has long been argued that the communication and substance of the curriculum cannot be disentangled, either by teacher or learner (Barnes 1976). In such a vein the first two English national history curricula were thick, pictureless, emotion-free, officially sanctioned government texts (DES 1991, 1995). They said much to teachers and learners about how politically powerful people seemed to lack vision or imagination in their educational views. Teachers and educational publishers mediated such curricula into more attractive, learning-led and child-friendly forms and the 2000 versions appear visually different (DfEE 1999a, b, c). Chapters 3 and 4 will argue that in subject-specific terms, this difference is largely cosmetic.

The traditional way of mediating curricula, whatever their appearance, has been through talk; especially teacher-talk. This remains a most powerful way for children to learn. During recent research we asked 120 primary aged children to rank the activities that they perceived helped them to learn most in history. Trialling of the research tool produced a list of twenty activities for children to choose from. Whichever way the results were analysed 'listening to teacher' stayed clearly at the top of the list (Bage, Grisdale and Lister 1999 p. 29). Although this may reflect children's compulsory experience as well as individual preference, it provides hard evidence of a commonsense assumption. Teachers are the richest historical resource to which most children have access. Through the simplest of technologies, namely talk, teachers are also in the best position to mediate historical information for learners.

This is not to claim that children's learning in history should only consist of listening to adults. It is to argue that talk is pre-eminent as an historical learning tool throughout the 4–14 age range, both to build learning through enquiry and to express it through communication. Since most children do not have easy, personalised access to professional or practising historians, it is teachers who need to model history: through the sorts of questions historians ask, the interpretations they make, the knowledge they desire and the specialist terminology they use. Papers referring to all these themes can be found in Chapters 5 and 6. Teachers talking for children, not at children, can achieve this, so long as children are motivated into then using historical language and thinking for themselves: literally, or orally 'making it their own'. These processes, of inducting learners into historical thinking and communicating, are riddled with the sorts of pedagogic decision-making expressed in our initial map. 'Differentiation vs standardisation' is a classic such question. The findings of the Nuffield History Project veered firmly towards the latter, arguing that whole class lessons and high quality teacher talk was a mainstay: 'much of our work necessarily stresses the importance of whole class teaching' (Fines and Nichol 1997 p. xiii). Equally, mere spoken exemplars are insufficient for long-term learning to occur. If they were, education might bloom through children simply watching television. Students' appropriate, individual engagement with history needs teaching by individuals empowered to take the sorts of pedagogic decisions described in our initial map.

Cooper (1998) for instance, demonstrates how historical enquiry can develop Y1 and Y2 children's speaking, listening and writing, especially when supported by a range of resources and experiences. In the context of a history topic on 'castles' and in preparation for a 'banquet' children wrote brief comparisons of clothes, extended descriptions, guest lists, invitations, menus, a programme of entertainments, jokes and stories. The preparation of information boards also demanded that they collated historical information, wrote up site notes from a visit and used historical vocabulary. The children's subsequent writing showed 'remarkable development from the original concept maps of castles . . . to the accurate and detailed site plans with information keys, and from the sites notes to the final extended writing' (ibid. p. 18). Realistic, varied language tasks, in the context of an interesting and motivating historical enquiry, developed more than the learning of a narrow range of historical skills.

Reynolds (1996) similarly describes various strategies, led by storytelling, groupwork and talk, to offer Y5/6 children the chance to show what they had learnt or not learnt from a local history enquiry and unit on 'Victorian Britain'. Such examples underscore the importance of teachers investing time in deeper learning, learning perhaps led by history but repaying the curriculum investment by developing literacy skills. Two boys, each experiencing different sorts of difficulty in learning, used historical photographs, role play and information from whole class activities to speak of their historical knowledge: 'David . . . illustrated his understanding of class, jobs, child workers: he also displayed judgement and empathy' while talk gave Karl 'a chance to express his opinions without them becoming entangled in his fears and frustrations with writing' (ibid. p. 175).

Wray and Lewis's (1997) work on non-fiction literacy heavily influenced the structure and content of this aspect of the English National Literacy Project, which abounds with examples of historical reading and writing (see Chapter 7 and Bage 1999a Chapter 9). Analysing how a class of 8 year olds compared conflicting accounts of the Norman Conquest prompted Wray and Lewis to argue that elements of historical thinking such as interpretations, enquiry and communication meld together in practice:

> The nature of historical records is such that it is almost impossible for there not to be a 'point of view' in the writing. As any Black South African, American Indian, or even Scot, will testify, what counts as history is almost always told from the point of view of the victors. Children need to be introduced to this idea by studying contrasting texts.
>
> (1997 p. 111)

Although such an idea is a mainstay of much history learning in secondary schools, the introduction of the national curriculum put teachers of all age ranges under enormous pressure to conform to the 'hurry along curriculum' (Dadds 1998): teaching for coverage, rather than learning in depth. It could be argued that such superficiality is as much a result of ineffective pedagogy as overcrowded curricula, and the historical examples scattered throughout this book show that historical learning was far from exemplary before the national curriculum. On the other hand there are good reasons to think carefully about what current curricula are encouraging in children's communication of history. A reasonably large sample of children's writing in history from ten primary schools across the country was analysed in a recent research project which I helped to lead. Despite none of the schools being considered as failing or at risk by OFSTED inspections, the research team were uniformily surprised by the following, bald finding. However the data was analysed, at least two thirds of the writing stuck into children's books or folders for history was superficial, closed, mechanical and basically undemanding. It reflected the aspirations of neither the history nor the English national curricula and was nowhere near fulfilling the textually varied ambitions of the national literacy strategy or framework (Bage, Grisdale and Lister 1999 pp. 18–21). The following comment can be read in parallel with this. It typifies many KS3 teachers' feelings about how curricula force learners into superficial experiences.

> I can't afford to give much more than this week to Thomas Becket. And anyway that's too much, because we've only got two weeks until the end of term . . . We're supposed to be doing the origins of parliament and the legacy of the Middle Ages . . . How do I get all that done in such a small space of time? . . . I'll probably show them a video of the Peasant's Revolt, or something.
>
> (Cooper and McIntyre 1996 p. 101)

The same, longitudinal research project showed how some teachers of history and English wanted to transform central curricula: to offer their students a more varied and motivating learning experience than they themselves had experienced at school, whatever the national curriculum demanded. For instance, interviews and lesson observations revealed one particular history teacher's 'willingness to allow lessons to be shaped on occasions by students' interests rather than the particular learning outcomes she has pre-planned' (ibid. p. 89). The 'communication and organisation' of learning history can therefore move beyond communicating and organising mere words, or even knowledge. It can extend to learning interpersonal and intrapersonal skills (Gardner 1993), even perhaps to developing 'emotional literacy'. This idea is:

> . . . not only about the ability to recognize our feelings and express them appropriately. It also involves questioning our attachment to a particular emotional experience and 're-framing' that experience in order to perceive it differently and, therefore, let go of our attachment to that emotion.
>
> (Askew and Carnell 1998 p. 29)

Do the emotions really have much to do with learning history, particularly as students grow older and more used to the varying demands of school? Research, scholarship and experience suggest that they do. The typically 'depersonalised' voice of historical information and textbooks, for instance, means that such texts are demonstrably harder to read for students than dialogues or narratives, with their attendant individualism (e.g. Wishart 1986, see also Chapter 5, Chapter 7) Recent, small-scale but in-depth research with American High School students likewise argued that history texts written by an author 'made visible', through techniques such as first-person writing and revelations of the writer's self, were more engaging historically and literally: 'history written as a "good story" invites readers to care about the subject with the prospect of deeper understanding . . . the introduction of a visible author did indeed seem to draw students closer to the information in the text' (Paxton 1997 p. 246). Research in KS3 history classrooms in English schools formalised a common tacit assumption by teachers and learners that effective teaching and learning involves 'a complex knowledge of the ways in which social, cognitive and affective aspects of classroom inter-action contributed to teaching and learning outcomes' (Cooper and McIntyre 1996 p. 118). Emotions matter in all classrooms, but learning about emotions matters especially *through* history and *in* history. Bruner surveyed twentieth century epistemology and education with scientific and poetic eyes, through narrative as well as paradigmatic knowledge (Bruner 1986). As history teachers and curriculum designers we should take to heart what he reveals about the nature and importance of historical learning:

> While the hard-nosed science professors were decrying the softness of the 'soft subjects' [such as history] Europe marched off to war once again – acting out the historical-social studies-literary stories that were presumed only to be 'enriching the mind'. Surely we could do better at understanding ourselves and our mad lurchings? Poison gas and Big Berthas might be the deadly fruits of verifiable science, but the impulse to use them grew out of those stories we tell ourselves. So should we not try to understand their power better, to see how stories and historical accounts are put together and what there is about them that leads people either to live together or to maim and kill each other?
>
> (Bruner 1996 p. 90)

'Learning history' cannot simplistically stop adults repeating the errors of the past, even though American students, English schoolchildren and their parents would like to believe that it can (Vansledright 1997; Bage, Grisdale and Lister 1999). What it may perhaps achieve is to educate individual humans to under-stand some errors, or handle uncertainties, in more emotionally, practically and cognitively civilised ways, than the alternative of ignorance offers.

2   Teaching History

Most people don't want what you and your colleagues think of as history –
the sort you get in books – because they don't know how to deal with it.
Personally, I've every sympathy – with them that is. I've tried to read a few
history books myself and while I may not be clever enough to enroll in your
classes, it seems to me that the main problem is this: they all assume you've
read most of the other history books already.

(Barnes 1998 pp. 70–1)

Mapping the Questions

Underlying Questions About How History Teaching
Adheres to predicted plans and objectives or responds to
    children's needs?   *Governance Issues*
Interacts with the whole child or only the student?   *Issues of Diversity*
Standardises or differentiates pedagogy and materials?   *Media Issues*
Is perceived as technical delivery or moral art?   *Values-led Issues*
Challenges or implements a school's stated aims for
    learning history?   *Democratic Issues*
Promotes transmission or analysis of historical knowledge? *Cognitive Issues*
Emphasises personal interpretation or social control?   *Social Issues*

This book offers a map of educational history based upon the premise that
teaching involves the incessant making of decisions. Decisions demanded by
learners can appear straightforward or even trivial: 'is this the right answer?' or
'but why I can't I work with my friend?' Others challenge the curriculum's worth:
'why do we learn about dead people?' Many request information or feedback on
a history task in hand: 'is this a good book for Tudors?' or 'what are the people
doing in this picture?' Classrooms are awash with such questions. Like the
goldfish's water as it swims round the bowl, the decision making they demand can
become invisible for teachers and learners.

   The quality of history learning and teaching at a local level, where immediate
decisions are made, is also defined by how such questions are answered. For
underlying them all are crucial and deeper decisions. These decisions rest upon
practicalities, such as the classroom resources and curriculum time available, for

teaching is a practical activity that builds understanding with people. The decisions also rest upon a host of deeper values and beliefs: of the teachers and learners concerned, of the school and community in which they work and of the government which, in the English case at least, heavily influences the curriculum taught.

Teachers in lessons are frequently faced with deciding, often in a split second 'Do I adhere to my predicted plans and objectives or respond to children and change something?' Answering such a question requires a very practical morality. If it is obvious, for instance, that a class of 6 year olds are taking far longer than anticipated to work out 'who might have used these old artefacts?', the concomitant teaching decisions must balance practicality and professionalism. Practically, it may mean that the children no longer have time to see the video which shows a Victorian household. Professionally, the decision has to be made about whether this particular handling of artefacts is going to result in 'better' learning if it takes twice as long, and whether it is going to be more worthwhile than the activities it displaces. Such decisions about what constitutes 'better' learning derive from values. The teacher may express values in her planning, emphasising for instance the importance of achieving measurable objectives. The school may express values in a policy statement, for instance desiring that children learn history from a wide range of firsthand experiences. The government may express values in curriculum documents, for instance by setting targets. Children also express values: some may esteem watching a video higher than handling old objects, or prefer PE to history. The job of teaching is not to 'follow' any of these particular dictates, for as in this case 'dictates' often end up being contradictory or irreconcilable. The practical and moral task of the teacher is to reconcile such demands where possible, and to be decisive about where it is not.

Such examples can be replicated across age ranges and across the questions posed in our 'map'. When a class is studying the life and times of Henry VIII and a 10 year old cries at a husband's cruelty, does the history teacher mark that down as an immature analysis of an historical problem; or remind himself that this child lives in a violent family? Does studying slavery in the British Empire 'feel' the same to teachers and learners in multicultural and monocultural classes? How teachers answer such questions depends perhaps upon whether we 'interact with the whole child or only the student' and how we 'standardise or differentiate pedagogy and materials'. In better schools, teachers do not feel alone in such decision making because they have colleagues with whom to talk questions over, and active policies or guidelines to help them. Awareness of such policies can improve classroom practice, though their written existence in a filing cabinet does not. For instance many school policies aim to promote equality of opportunity in history: yet does the history curriculum children actually experience in classrooms raise questions about gender, class or cultural disadvantage? History teachers have to decide, in our everyday practice, how to 'challenge or implement their school's stated aims for learning history'.

Similarly with questions on our map as to whether teaching 'promotes transmission or analysis of historical knowledge' and 'emphasises personal interpretation or social control'. Most history teachers develop a personal style by individualsing our teaching language, resources, organisation and ethos. In the same school it is easy to find one teacher telling students what 'castles were for' or what 'the Industrial Revolution was', prior to examining historical evidence; and another teacher starting the other way round, using the evidence first to stimulate interest. Neither approach is automatically right or wrong: such teachers are merely taking different routes through some of our map's key areas.

Their capacity to do so is essential, as is their commonsense, organisational abilities, interpersonal and communication skills. For teaching is, touching upon the last of our map's questions, both 'technical delivery and moral art'. The practical and personal demands teaching makes and the knowledge it entails require a high level of technical proficiency, at least when done well. Yet the interpretative nature of the subject matter and the human relationships involved in history education entail creativity and moral decisions. History is about other worlds and classrooms create other worlds, worlds different in important ways from the societies in which they exist. Leading learners willingly into such worlds is a moral and creative act of the highest order: one that cannot be achieved without the exercise of skilful, sensitive and practical moralities. At least that is what this theorist would like you to believe: but what does the history of history teaching tell us?

The History and Image of History Teaching

What does it mean and what has it meant to teach about this thing called history? According to one interpretation, systematic attempts to teach history as a named and distinct school subject in England start with the Renaissance. These originated as the preserve of the old and privileged: classically dead, white, European men.

> The study of history was advocated in the period up to 1660 for nobles and gentlemen, both on educational grounds and also as a class distinction. Furthermore it was considered that history required a sound judgement as to affairs . . . Such a conception necessarily involved the postponement of historical studies to a more mature age than the school, and even a riper age than the University courses.
>
> (Foster Watson 1909)

The commercial expansion of the book trade through printing also created a market for history, related not just to schools but to what in modern terms we might call 'leisure-led' or lifelong leaning:

> It was the pride of London citizens that first gave rise to chronicles published in the vernacular . . . Holinshed . . . Grafton . . . Stow . . . Speed . . . Camden . . . Holland . . . The common reader passed on from chronicles and the ubiquitous Book of Martyrs to North's translation of Plutarch's Lives designed for the 'common sort', and eventually more philosophical works such as Raleigh's History of the World.
>
> (Simon 1966 pp. 385–6)

A potential theme to the modern history of history teaching is, then, uncomfortably Whiggish: that history has in the last few centuries gradually moved from an aristocratic, leisurely and elitist pursuit to a comprehensive compulsion in which 4 to 14 year olds in English schools are forced to participate.

Although this appears attractive, history is more complex. In our contemporary sense the history teacher as a professional is an invention of the modern period. Equally it is possible to find numerous ancient and medieval instances of history being taught about through story, both officially and unofficially (e.g. Bage 1999a). Thomas Cromwell's son Gregory, for instance, was educated by a tutor in the 1530s. A typical day started with Mass then moved on to reading, translation of the classics, reading of historical chronicles and writing. The afternoon reflected many modern primary school curricular divisions and contained music, PE and story-telling. It was for 'playing upon the lute and virginals, for riding (when his tutor recounted some Roman or Greek history by the way which the boy retailed again in the form of a story), for hawking, hunting and shooting with the long bow' (Simon 1966 pp. 155–6).

'Unofficial' educational histories have also always existed, independent of formal schooling and rooted in popular culture:

> The first histories, in medieval Europe as in ancient Greece, were the ballads ... war memorials ... giving an epic quality to what in the original event may have been a comparatively minor skirmish. Ballads served as mnemonics in recitations of genealogy and ... the learning of dynastic history.
>
> (Samuel 1994 p. 22)

Samuel cites musical traditions, painters, engravers, seamstresses, masons, carvers, goldsmiths, jurors and artisan guilds as similar guardians of popular tradition and custom. Indeed 'memory' has been a driving force throughout European culture, since the transition of ancient Greek poetry and Roman law from oral into literate forms. Cultures may have deployed the 'art of memory' differently but historians have shown how past human societies relied in various ways upon memory and narrative to create their present (e.g. Ashe 1990; Hutton 1993; White 1987). As was argued in Chapter 1, the modern urge formally to teach and learn history conforms to this over-arching imperative. It is also a mistake to see 'education' in a modern, school-centred sense as the only method of teaching history.

> In the Middle Ages spectacle had been quite fundamental to the dissemination of sacred history . . . street theatre .. with its banners, tabernacles and crosses and the open-air perambulating stages . . . procession ... annual turn-outs and open-air demonstrations of the artisan trades.
>
> (Samuel 1994 p. 28)

One modern equivalent to such medieval multimedia is screen-based history embedded in television, film and game. Speaking of the American market, this analyst described how such media tended to ignore or misrepresent the work of historians and history teachers: 'At best, then, within popular imagery the history teacher is little but a skilled lecturer, repeating truths that were established before he or she retold them' (Polan 1996 p. 245). The popularity of process-based history programmes such as 'Time Team' in English television, in which archeologists and historians work against the clock to construct an historical interpretation of a site or event, at least move beyond the idea of history-as-lecture. Yet the following comments still apply on both sides of the Atlantic and are pertinent to history educators:

> Conceptions of the historical past are rampant in popular culture, but conceptions of historians are few and far between. History as a professional activity appears to have little place in public consciousness precisely at a moment (the moment we often term 'post-modernity') in which the question of the potentially public nature of history is of burning pertinence. The discipline of history may well need to examine the visibility or, more likely, the invisibility of its image so that it does not blithely continue a descent into cultural irrelevance.
>
> (Polan 1996 p. 255)

Even the history of 'official school history' is not as straightforward as it seems. It is easy to read Victorian history textbooks as promoting closed, regulated views. This extract from a textbook of around 1870 typifies the perceived dominant style:

> Who was Henry VIII?
> Son of Henry VII.
>
> What was his character?
> As a young man he was bluff, generous, right royal and very handsome.
>
> How was he when he grew older?
> He was bloated, vain, cruel and selfish.
>
> (quoted in Gosden 1969 p. 50)

These crude instructional techniques sound alien to modern educational ears and were used to promote imperialist notions of history through textbooks and teaching (e.g. Humphries 1981 p. 40). Equally such moralising, though simplistic, may have contributed to independent thought, just as the 2000 English history national curriculum attempts to generate thinking skills and critical awareness. A study of over 150 nineteenth century history school textbooks concluded that:

> The concern with morality was by no means confined to the imagination of the textbook writers. It actually existed as a force in society and was exploited politically by Gladstone among others. Springing as it did from the

evangelical movement, it was not a comfortable or conformist force for it placed emphasis on individual judgement about the concerns of the nation and set standards above mere convenience by which statesmen of the past and present should be judged. These standards underly many of the opinions which are to be found in history textbooks.

(Chancellor 1970 pp. 140–1)

Nor is a textbook read automatically a lesson learnt. Speaking of his Edwardian schooling this man described enduring, but resisting childhood's official history with what he learnt unofficially. According to his testimony, imperialist history:

> ... didn't make much impression on me ... It went into my brain and I stored the facts because you had to, but patriotism never struck me as being very clever. See, I'd read Tom Paine ... His outlook was towards being a citizen of the world ... that gave me a broader outlook than the school history books, and that was when I was twelve years old.
>
> (quoted in Humphries 1981 p. 44)

The fact that other men and women of similar age describe refusing to conform to school standards in affairs of religion, discipline or respect for empire and monarchy (ibid.) shows that independently-minded children and teachers did not simply accept textbook history at face value. Opposition and indifference to British imperialism has manifested itself throughout modern educational history and was 'reflected in the study and teaching of history' (Aldrich 1988 p. 35). Imperialism's educational proponents anyway sowed the seeds for their own historical opposition. Seeley was a classical scholar turned Cambridge professor of imperial history, and a central figure in early twentieth century attempts to popularise historical understandings and appreciation of imperialism. As such he opened one of his volumes with the educational ambition that history 'should not merely gratify the reader's curiosity about the past, but modify his view of the present and his forecast of the future' (ibid. p. 27). Although such a statement is not far removed from many late twentieth century English parental views of the purpose of school history (Bage, Grisdale and Lister 1999), Seeley also elaborated that 'if this maxim be sound, the history of England ought to end with something that might be called a moral' (Aldrich 1988 p. 27). The identification of history with a search for moral lessons contains within itself the possibility, indeed the likelihood, that different interpretations of the same events will open them to contested moral judgements: in this case to argue 'against' as well as 'for' imperialism. Seeley is perhaps not as distant from modernity as many educators would like to believe. Nor did teaching an imperial school history automatically equate to teaching a monocultural history. A *School History of England* (Fletcher and Kipling 1911) contained simplistic and unquestioning justifications of the British empire for use with junior classes (Leinster-Mackay 1988 p. 63), with which contemporary values find it easy to disagree. It also opens with a poem that celebrates emotional and multicultural views of English history. In this the Thames, personified, tells readers its 'River's Tale'. Reminding children that in former days 'England was joined to the continent', it also sketches an England, a London and a Greenwich that had in previous periods been multicultural and itself enslaved by empires:

> While down at Greenwich for slaves and tin
> The tall Phoenician ships stole in,
> And North Sea war-boats, painted and gay,
> Flashed like dragon-flies Erith way;
> And Norseman and Negro and Gaul and Greek
> Drank with the Britons in Barking Creek . . .
> But the Roman came with a heavy hand,
> And bridged and roaded and ruled the land,
> And the Roman left and the Danes blew in –
> And that's where your history books begin!
>
> (Fletcher and Kipling 1911 pp. 9–10)

If the history of history teaching tells us anything, it is that neither history nor teaching are entirely predictable.

Models of 'Quality' in History Teaching

At first sight the past can appear unitary to the present, its very 'pastness' marking it off as complete: yet those who lived in the past when it was the present embodied similar confusions or controversies to those that you and I experience, as we read this book or practice our craft. Elements of argument and uncertainty about history and education are as old as they are inevitable, leading to differing perspectives of 'quality'. For instance this female history teacher raises 'modern' issues of resourcing, specialism, curriculum, pedagogy and class size:

> It is time for history teachers to assert themselves and claim for their subject a due amount of consideration. For history is suffering . . . from the modern tendency to sacrifice English subjects to the demands of science and modern languages . . . English history must be continued to 1901 . . . local history must not be forgotten . . . history teaching should, as a general rule, be entirely in the hands of history specialists . . . It is only the trained student of history who has the sense of historical proportion, which is at the bottom of all really successful history teaching . . . small classes should be taught . . . It is perfectly easy to interest a class of forty, fifty or sixty . . . but twenty-five is the outside limit of a class in which an individual can be really taught.

She was writing nearly a century ago (Howard 1905 pp. 367–8). Meanwhile this woman teacher reflected upon her experience of teaching history to 'a class of little children' using the locality of Exeter in which she found herself. In doing so she reveals how her practice anticipated teaching and learning theories that moderns (e.g. Applebee 1978; Bage 1999a) have since advanced in more detail:

I suppose it is true of all children that at first the people about whom they hear are real, whether they belong to fairy tales or history. Then comes a time of unconscious selection, and the child separates into classes those who before were grouped together. He has nothing certain to go upon: his experience is so limited . . . Unconsciously he is feeling for some point of contact with life . . . surely this point of contact is most easily and successfully found in local history.

(Shorto 1908 p. 499)

She also offered a defintion of 'quality' which, given its prominent place in this book's forthcoming chapters, is irresistibly attractive:

I am quite sure that one of the reasons why even careful teaching produces such poor results is that the imagination is not sufficiently appealed to . . . a girl whom I once knew, after much searching in the dark corners of memory, confused the prophet Jonah with a mysterious personage whom she called Jonah Arc and who, she declared, led the French. So anything that helps to stimulate and develop the imagination is of value, and I claim for local history the greatest importance in this respect.

(ibid.)

Jumping a century, Alexander (1995) brilliantly explains how in the case of primary schooling, such controversies and cultures cannot be consigned to a ghetto marked 'past': they live on into the present. Drawing on the educational history of the last two centuries he demonstrates how:

Ideologies do not come in single file, one replacing another, but compete, interact and continue in juxtaposition. Some are modified, some are driven, temporarily or permanently, underground, minority viewpoints become majority ones, and vice versa. Different ideologies continue to influence the system in different ways and to differing degrees.

(ibid. pp. 16–17)

In particular the traditions of 'progressive' and 'elementary' education, rooted in the eighteenth and nineteenth centuries, trace not just the foundations of current primary educational debate but its very architectural, organisational and intellectual superstructure (ibid. pp. 275–88). As a school subject, history is part of that fabric. Its past and present are acted out in classrooms and schools, by scholars and teachers, using textbooks and blackboards for learning and curricula. Such practical, contextual elements are reflected in our map of educational polarities and in this book's subject matter. History is also, though, a thinking and developing discipline which extends far beyond schools into the social and intellectual life of communities. This interplay of school subject with thinking discipline is one of the most distinctive strands of discussions concerning quality in history teaching and we will use it to tie together this chapter.

Farmer and Knight (1995 p. 1) succinctly summarised the recent history of history teaching in an attempt to move beyond 'stereotypical' views of 'what history teaching was like four or five decades ago.' Such ambition becomes ever more important with every new political pressure for educators to conform to centralised curricula. For if teachers of history are to preserve curriculum space within which to exercise professional autonomy, an autonomy which this book argues is essential to improving learning and practice, then clearer recognition is needed that extant educational traditions weigh far heavier than any new initiative, or reform of the moment. The 'new' history of the 1970s, government-sponsored curriculum projects of the 1970s and 1980s, 1990s national curricula in history, national grids for learning, national literacy and numeracy strategies: these were and often are important and worthwhile innovations. They are also episodic, even in the context of a child's school career and certainly in the case of a teacher practising pedagogy over several decades. Each should be judged not just on its merits, rather than its claims; but over a period of time and against the sort of enduring traditions and issues which Alexander (1995), Farmer and Knight (1995) and this book sketch. It could be argued that a foundation of 'quality' in history teaching is that it employs a history of itself to inform its judgements: otherwise how can it claim to say anything either historical, or educational?

Farmer and Knight's discussion of quality takes place against such a background. It also reminds us of the still-tentative nature of research about teaching and learning in history:

> In theory, the best way of identifying quality teaching is to say that it leads to greater-than-expected gains in learning . . . The recent experience of National Curriculum testing in England shows that this approach is full of technical problems and that it is of no help at present . . . any account of effective history teaching will not be based on compelling research evidence.
>
> (Farmer and Knight 1995 pp. 27–8)

At this point you as reader, even me as writer, might be tempted to throw our book away. If research cannot tell us about quality, why read it or do it?

This depends what we mean by research. In subsequent sentences Farmer and Knight venture that their 'own experience and the literature on teaching and learning' sourced their 'twelve pointers to effective history teaching'. They need not have been so apologetic about lacking quantitative data. Judgements about learning, descriptions of practice and scholarly arguments all count as 'research' if they meet criteria developed by one of the keenest twentieth century thinkers on education, research and history. Lawrence Stenhouse defined research as 'systematic and sustained inquiry, planned and self-critical, which is subjected to public criticism and to empirical tests where these are appropriate' (Stenhouse 1981 p. 113). This view not only leaves the way open for you as reader, and me as writer, to consider our practice as research data, and to open it to research scrutiny. It also places the onus on researchers to make themselves more accessible and answerable to practitioners. Stenhouse concluded the article just referred to with the following words:

> 'Teachers must inevitably be intimately involved in the research process and ... researchers must justify themselves to practitioners, not practitioners to researchers.'

(ibid. p. 113)

It is a valid test for us as readers to place research, governmental claims, policies and propaganda, not so much at the centre of our world view as in a focused, sharply critical spotlight. Experience and scholarship suggest we should not jump onto a single, bandwagon view of quality in teaching and let it take us where it wills. As a professional alternative we can root ourselves in living educational traditions (McIntyre 1981; Elbaz 1991) helping us carefully and sceptically pick over the trinkets hawked by educational bandwagons. Scholarship and experience can help us decide what, if anything, we choose to trade from them, or whether to send the wagon packing to the next bunch of suckers. In such a spirit the following summaries of 'quality' in history teaching are offered, all developed within the 1990s framework of English and Welsh national history curricula. Following earlier arguments, how these may contribute to your particular educational history in the twenty-first century depends upon what course you are setting in your teaching and learning; and on what obstacles your route has to navigate.

Farmer and Knight (see Figure 2.1)

Although framed in the context of KS3/4, both these writers have considerable experience of research and teaching in KS1/2; their 'pointers' can inform history thinking across the age ranges. They are also premised upon promoting active learning in the sense that participants are actively intellectually engaged in the process of history.

The Nuffield Primary History Project (NPHP)

The Nuffield Primary History Project commenced in 1991 as a funded, major attempt to improve historical teaching and learning; many of the team members also had decades of previous experience in the field. A unique and inspirational aspect of the initiative was that most of its writings drew from reflection upon practice by teachers and researcher–teachers, across the age ranges 5–14. In this it mirrored some of the aspirations expressed by Stenhouse (1981) for alterations to the research-practice relationship in education. The author was involved in the later stages through dissemination and testing of the NPHP's principles with Cambridgeshire schools. At the time of writing the project continues to explore the relationships between history and literacy in particular (see Figure 2.2). The tragic death of Professor John Fines in 1999 robbed the NPHP, and the world of history education, of one its finest practitioners.

Figure 2.1 Twelve pointers to effective history teaching

1 Curriculum management	Learners need consistent expectations throughout a school to achieve high quality history – an issue of curriculum leadership and management.
2 Classroom management	High quality learning means stimulating new and more complex thinking, leading to more questions, conversations, etc. A teacher's classroom management skills need to be able to cope with this.
3 Teachers' manner	Cullingford (1995) found that learners valued highly teachers with: humour, organisation, a real interest in learning and communication.
4 Subject understanding	Learners need teachers to use and understand history processes in pedagogy, and to know lots of history to aid differentiation.
5 Clarity of purpose	Effective teachers clarify and communicate the purposes of the subject, curriculum and lessons and discuss these with learners. This stimulates metacognition – learners knowing about knowing.
6 Key concepts	History has two sorts of key concept: procedural (e.g. chronology, evidence, causation, change, continuity, interpretations) and substantive (e.g. church, civilisation, revolution). Learners' existing understandings of both are the starting point for effective teaching.
7 Metacognition	Metacognition is stimulated by appropriate classroom organisation and teaching styles: learners being challenged to communicate understandings and take responsibility for organising their own learning.
8 Depth	Effective teachers translate curricular requirements, judging which historical aspects are most profitable for learners to pursue in the time available.
9 Teaching strategically	Effective teachers have a range of strategies at their disposal, ensuring that children experience a balance over time (see 'perspectives meeting from east and west' below).
10 Assessment of learning	Assessment needs to be specific, positive and offer learners ways of improving historical performance – to be about history, not just presentation or behaviour.
11 Going beyond 'the' text	Effective history teaching ends up combining a variety of texts – emphasising the importance of diverse sources and interpretations.
12 Differentiation	Setting open-ended, focused and stepped tasks and using mixed ability groups are classic differentiation strategies – but differentiation in history can be an issue of gender, cultural or ethnic background as well as pure 'attainment'.

Figure 2.2 Five principles from the Nuffield Primary History Project (Fines and Nichol 1997 pp. vii–xiii)

1	**Questioning**	Pupils work like historians: 'History is about asking and answering questions, and above all, getting children to ask questions.'
2	**Challenges**	Materials and questions should challenge learners 'to persist, to speculate, to make connections, to debate issues, to understand the past from the inside.' Open questions and real enquiries fuel these qualities.
3	**Integrity and economy of sources**	Often, just one source is used at a time: 'We teach real history, so that we use authentic sources of history. More wide-ranging and useful questions can be asked of a few well chosen sources, than from an unfocused jumble.'
4	**Depth**	'Real historical knowledge, even at primary level, demands study in depth. Only by getting deeply inside the past can pupils develop expertise and confidence.'
5	**Accessibility**	Pedagogic craft knowledge is essential: 'We make history accessible to all children by starting with what children can do ... using a wide variety of teaching approaches, including well paced whole-class teaching, co-operative pair work and group work.'

'East meets West': Brooks, Aris and Perry (1993) and Suffolk LEA (1991, 1995)

In a book drawing together many practical suggestions on the teaching of history 5–16, Brooks acknowledged the usefulness of the introduction of the national curriculum to education in Wales. In similar vein to the present discussion, teachers of history were also urged to look beyond it. 'It is up to effective teachers to use their professional skills to translate this [a national curriculum] into a worthwhile and meaningful experience for each of their pupils' (Brooks, Aris and Perry 1993 p. 96). One approach to 'translation' is to deploy a range of teaching and learning strategies. Aris, a museums education officer, offered a useful list of these in the same book. Her work mirrored similar syntheses independently and simultaneously arrived at in eastern England by the Suffolk Humanities Advisory Team, of which the author was a member (Suffolk LEA 1991, 1995). National curricula in England, Wales and perhaps elsewhere, may appear in policy terms to constrain the history curriculum; but can as easily be a creative prompt for its diversification at classroom level. The following table summarises some of the pedagogic strategies or starting points available to teachers of history 4–14 and developed within such national curricula (see Figure 2.3).

Figure 2.3 Teaching and learning activities and resources for History KS1–3
(synthesised from Brooks, Aris and Perry 1993, Suffolk LEA 1991,
1995 p. 28)

Examples of Contexts	Examples of Activities or Resources
Whole class teaching and large group teaching – or individual and paired work	*storytelling* *discussion* *exposition* *illustrated talks* *group reading* *demonstration*
Contact with teacher or other adults	*interviews with experts or enthusiasts* *discussion with friends, family or others* *oral history inside or outside of school* *guides and guided tours*
Individual, paired, group or classwork using reproduced primary sources	*documents* *media and other printed sources* *visual sources* *spoken word* *songs and music* *maps and plans* *investigating in a library, archive or local history centre*
Individual, paired, group or classwork using secondary sources	*reference and information books, pamphlets or others* *school text books* *guidebooks and information boards* *television or film* *ICT* *fictional and imaginative writing*
Learners presenting to a group or whole class	*speech or lecture* *storytelling* *description* *argument* *recount*
Discussion in pairs small groups or whole class	*analysing evidence* *brainstorming* *problem-solving* *planning activities* *formal debate* *round table* *hot seating* *devil's advocate* *panel discussions*
Using ICT	*researching via the worldwide web* *researching using CD ROMs* *word-processing* *interrogating or compiling databases* *taking part in simulations* *designing or manipulating images*
Participating in historical drama	*imaginative play* *role playing and improvisation* *re-enactment*

Examples of Contexts	Examples of Activities or Resources
	plays and playlets
	theatre in education
	tableaux and mime
	dance and movement
Investigating artefacts	*reproduction artefacts*
	pictures of artefacts
	artefacts from home and school
	antique and junk shops
	children's own artefacts
	high status artefacts in museums
	fragments of artefacts
Investigating historical landscape or buildings	*using plans, maps or atlases*
	photographs
	memories
	placenames
	fieldwork
	following or designing historical trails
	surveying and measuring
Handling or analysing statistical data	*graphs*
	tables
	spreadsheets
Analysing historical art, architecture, inscriptions or statues	*illustrations*
	paintings, drawings and engravings
	posters and adverts
	private and public architecture
	memorials
Analysing or creating sources from film	*still photography from media, family or other sources*
	films with historical themes
	children's leisure and educational television
	adult television
	cartoons
	adverts
	archive film for information, propaganda or news
Experiencing live or recorded oral and aural sources	*presenting historical talk or music*
	listening to historical talk or music
	listening and talking to expert visitors
	investigating through oral history
	conducting interviews and opinion polls
Fieldwork	*in the locality of the school*
	a visit to an historic site or building
	a visit to a museum
Archaeology	*classroom simulations*
	visiting digs
	media reports
	viewing and displaying finds
Practical tasks	*making models or replicas*
	constructing wall or museum displays
	collage
	models, sculpture and other 3D representations

Brown (1995)

Although writing for history subject and department leaders in secondary schools, Brown's analysis of what makes for effective history leadership has much to say about the effective teaching of history in primary schools. First, and whilst discussing 'assuring quality', he suggests that 'collaborative management is the best way of assuring successful student learning of history' (Brown 1995 p. 47). Partners in this enterprise include teachers, pupils or students, learning assistants, parents and guardians and the local community. Second, although externally measured results matter via SATs, exams or inspections 'quality in learning cannot be defined on the basis of a single criterion' (ibid. p. 51). Third:

> Learning history cannot be reduced to a series of elements of knowledge and skill. It depends on the development of a complex weave of interrelated objectives and components that interact with students . . . Teachers have to work with this uncertainty in student learning and no pat answers or alleged conclusive proof can resolve totally this continuing dilemma.
>
> (ibid. p. 53)

Fourth, 'teaching history as a performing art picks up the dynamic and fluid quality of the classroom experience . . . it allows a focus on the whole process of learning history rather than, as we so often do, breaking it down into its component parts' (ibid. p. 65). Lastly in this synthesis and based upon some research conducted in history classrooms, ambitious or 'Hoshin' goals need planning for in history, grounded in seven principles (see Figure 2.4).

Figure 2.4 Planning outrageous goals for history learning – grounded in seven principles (adapted slightly from Brown 1995 pp. 55–6)

1	**Plan for participation**	History's place in the curriculum relates to and enacts whole-school aims. Unless all teachers of history in a school are led into participation in this process, progress will be limited.
2	**Plan for empowerment**	Within this framework, space needs to be negotiated for individual teachers to lead initiatives.
3	**Attack causes**	Root causes of poor learning are identified, through detailed discussion with students and teachers. Students are then asked asked to take more responsibility for their own historical learning.
4	**Take risks**	Real improvement by definition entails higher risk, working in areas where learners and teachers feel less secure. An atmosphere mixing challenge and support is needed for this to occur.
5	**The key is quality**	Clarifications of quality will be encouraged by dialogue about 1–4 above. High expectations are essential.
6	**Communicate, communicate, then communicate some more**	Managers, teachers, learners and the parents, guardians and community of those involved in a school need to know about history learning if they are to extend it. This means consistently communicating history's aims, means and achievements.
7	**Focus on process**	'Effective outcomes follow effective processes.' This is true for teachers as much as learners, requiring self-monitoring from both.

Claire (1995)

We have mentioned on several occasions the centrality of values to educational history, which Claire has clarified and embodied in powerful ways. Drawing on personal experience as well as professional knowledge, Claire links thinking underlying the discipline of history to education at all levels. She reminds readers that lessons from historiography inform teaching, learning and the curriculum by linking history to the communities whose stories it claims to tell. British history isolated from world history, 'Whig' history's over-emphasis upon the inevitably of progress, the dangers of eurocentrism and imperialism, the male-centredness of much existing history and the vibrancy of 'history from below' in compensating for the imbalance of history sources: these are important ideas or principles for any age group (see Figure 2.5). In condensed form, Claire offers a values-led reminder for teachers of history that 'quality' depends upon historical content as well as form.

Figure 2.5 Arguments for inclusive history teaching (adapted from Claire 1996 pp. 6–10)

Because of '. . . the huge influence of the media, particularly television news, on children's interest in and knowledge about national and international issues . . . There are good arguments for a more inclusive history curriculum for the primary school.'

1 Children need to contextualise information received through the media in order to understand it better.
2 They [children] are interested anyway.
3 A Eurocentric and male-centred curriculum fails to prepare children adequately for life in the coming century.
4 A Eurocentric and male-centred curriculum is basically unjust and biased about the contributions and history of women and non-European people.
5 This limited curriculum continues to support sexism, racism and class misunderstanding by perpetuating outdated attitudes.
6 History develops the asking and answering of the same sort of questions which underpin critical literacy, citizenship and thinking skills.

Therefore Primary School history should take account of:

Race and ethnicity   To support the learning, self-esteem and identification with history of black and ethnic minority children.

To offer white children tangible, positive but critical perspectives on histories such as those of the English, Irish, etc.

To give black and white children non-Eurocentric approaches with which to understand the modern world and counteract ignorance and prejudice.

Gender   To counter sexism and marginalisation of women's contribution, as part of the education of boys.

To offer girls and boys positive but different role models and identities within their learning of history and therefore foster a sense of their own potential agency.

Class   To make sure that working-class children have a point of entry and identification with the content of history.

To empower children by challenging the view that change has always been the work of the rulers and the powerful.

To give children the opportunity to start learning about the difficult and painful paths towards democracy.

Conclusion

We have been discussing 'quality' in history teaching: but is the reality that our teaching is only as good as the learning children accomplished in our last history lesson? Although such an approach sounds impossibly pressurised, there is a sense in which this argument holds fast. It is difficult to judge teaching other than through observing its practice, just as it is impossible to judge art other than by looking at it, or music by hearing it, or literature by reading or listening to it. Teaching is a living process. This process leaves records such as children who have learnt, or written, or spoken or made things; but these point to the teachers we *were* when the records were made and not to the teachers *we are now*, in this living and thinking moment. The awful truth is that we have to reinvent ourselves and our teaching for every lesson; which explains why this writer suffers nightmares at the start of each school year. Am I still good enough: can I still teach?

A corollary of this performative aspect of quality in teaching is that we rarely attain perfection and never on a permanent basis. We may improve or regress, consolidate or revolutionise; but if quality is our aspiration we always have to rethink and renegotiate our aims in lessons, terms and years. Quality in pedagogy cannot be a stable state. Teaching therefore offers some of society's most challenging and rewarding work: what support can society offer in return?

Putting aside obvious answers such as money, status and productive political support, we will focus here upon teaching and learning to mirror our opening chapters. How, as teachers of history, can we can learn about and teach with quality? One approach is to remember that learning, as children or adults, relies upon more than discrete cognition. As Askew and Carnell recently argued:

> If the affective, social and spiritual aspects of learning are not taken into account, then learning may not take place, no matter how good the teaching. Teachers are taught how to teach. The assumption behind this is that if teachers know how to teach, then learning will automatically occur. We refute this.
>
> (1998 p. 167)

In the context of teachers' professional development, Day (1999) draws from extensive research and practice to summarise how learning from experience can be moved up a gear, into learning from development (see box opposite).

Teachers reading this can judge for themselves the extent to which they have experienced such conditions, either in preparation for teaching as a whole career or for the perhaps small part of professional life involved with the teaching of history. Curriculum leaders or managers of history might also like to consider how to meet at least some of these conditions as they support colleagues in their work. Meanwhile we conclude with insights from an interesting, perhaps inspiring American attempt to develop teachers of primary and secondary history.

The California History-Social Science Project (CH-SSP) is part of 'one of the most ambitious and large-scale efforts in the US in recent years to bring teachers

---

Some necessary conditions for developmental learning by teachers
(Day 1999 pp. 205–6)

- to connect with requirements at critical moments in teachers' development lives;
- to enable self-confrontation through reflection which raises questions about purposes, practices and contexts;
- extended critical engagement with peers and others;
- to connect educational knowledge with knowledge about education through partnerships and networks which bring together a range of stakeholders;
- to be part of an ongoing dialogue between teacher and the school which recognizes that the needs of the system and individual may not always coincide but will serve one another;
- to reflect participation in a range of different kinds of learning opportunities over time appropriate to need;
- to be focused upon classroom and school management, subject knowledge, broader intellectual, emotional commitment and vision needs;
- to be based upon a personal development plan owned and used as a review and planning means by each teacher over a career.

---

and the professoriate together over curriculum issues' (Seixas 1999 p. 319). Working in summer schools at ten college and university sites, the programme provides teachers with access to historical researchers working at universities; and lecturers and professors with access to experts in pedagogy and education. Its evaluator noticed in the course of his work that 'teachers and professors invoked the discourse of content and pedagogy frequently' (ibid. p. 320). Often, though not always they assumed that universities had most expertise in the former and schools in the latter. What came to concern the evaluator was how, perhaps arising from such assumptions, the mutual and beneficial relationships between understanding historical content and understanding pedagogy in history could be over-simplified or ignored. Here he describes a very experienced middle school teacher: 'for her the historian was the keeper of the content, whose work she supplements with strategies for content delivery.' Meanwhile an equally experienced history professor speculated that teachers 'are probably not accustomed to the kind of debates that we get in the professional circles which is a complete breakdown of narrative, of any kind of construction of reality and truth . . . I feel very uncomfortable in raising those sorts of concerns [with teachers]' (ibid. p. 321–2).

Such divides could, the American evaluator suggested, be bridged by thinking of history as 'doing the discipline'. This idea became common in English secondary schools during the 1970s and 1980s and at a policy level at least, has been well represented in the English national history curricula of the 1990s. 'Doing the discipline establishes a basis for teachers and professors to work together in a way which recognizes the expertise of historians, not as dispensers of fixed content, but as practitioners of a craft into which others are welcomed' (ibid. p. 328). Arguing in similar ways to the earlier work of Stenhouse (1975,

1981) on curriculum and teaching, Seixas shows how developing understandings of historical pedagogy and content are actually interdependent:

> There are two closely related aspects of 'doing the discipline' of history. The first is the critical reading of texts . . . The second is the construction of historical accounts. Although these tasks are often construed as jobs for historians alone, in fact teachers and students engage in similar processes, though often less consciously. Teachers read, select and edit texts that offer students accounts of the past. And, to the extent that these texts, and teachers' presentations of them, offer a coherent story, teachers also construct an account of the past for their students . . . historians, teachers and students are all involved in a roughly analogous process.
>
> (ibid. p. 328)

This process has been interpreted similarly by this author, working in England and across the 4–14 age range over the last two decades. I have come to the relatively simple conclusion that 'History is the construction and deconstruction of explanatory narratives about the past, derived from evidence and in answer to questions.' (Bage 1999a p. 33) Not just story, not just analysis, but a synthesis of both. In this vision teachers and learners become storytellers, of history stories told from and through the curriculum: a topic to which we now turn.

3   History and Curriculum

I do not believe that any two men, on what are called doctrinal points, think alike who think at all.

(Paine 1792 p. 293)

Mapping the Questions

Underlying Questions About How History Curricula

Are locally or nationally defined?	*Governance Issues*
Are interdisciplinary or subject specific?	*Issues of Diversity*
Advance multimedia or only written literacy skills?	*Media Issues*
Open adults' values to scrutiny or promote their acceptance?	*Values-led Issues*
Reveal or obscure the grounds for history's claims to value?	*Democratic Issues*
View history as a social activity or one pursued only in school?	*Cognitive Issues*
Are negotiated teacher to child or standardised?	*Social Issues*

As with many countries across the world, England has constructed a legislative framework for national school curricula. As with other countries, this framework stipulates fine details of history teaching and learning and promotes those stories which decision-makers want told. Coverage of content is mandated: for instance that between the ages of 7 and 11 children undertake a local history study, or are taught about a pre-1914 European turning point between the ages of 11 and 14. Learning objectives are set for different age ranges demanding, for example, that 5, 6 and 7 year olds should be 'taught how to identify different ways in which the past is represented' (DfEE 1999a p. 16).

In the face of such official prescription it is easy to conclude that English schools and teachers have little influence over the history curriculum: that navigational control over whether 'history curricula are locally or nationally defined' has been taken away from teachers. Indeed some of those in political control of curriculum policy are keen to promote such a perception: it enables them to pose as powerful in public media whilst identifying such power with a supposed 'national' good. Early in the last decade, for instance, political decision making over the English national curriculum in history helped certain journalists and politicians to portray themselves as 'saviours' of traditional school history:

A return to facts, events and traditional teaching in history was trumpeted last week when John MacGregor made his pronouncements on the national curriculum.

(*TES* 3 August 1990 'McGregor fails to ruffle history critics')

History teaching is set for a shake-up after a Minister attacked the 'silly Sixties-based approach' yesterday. School minister Baroness Blatch condemned one text book, used in many schools, which purports to teach historical 'skills'. . . A letter sent from 10 Downing Street on behalf of the Prime Minister . . . signals a back to basics. There was 'no dispute' that history had been the victim of an 'insidious attack' by progressive educationists, it said.

(*Daily Mail* 15 October 1992 'This history is bunk')

Glib assumptions that curricula could be nationalised at the wave of a political wand led to dangerous complacencies, many still current as this book is being written. One is that a centrally standardised curriculum can be 'correct' for all children and communities. Another is that the matter of 'whose history?' can be democratically answered by central imposition. A third is that teachers have only to implement this curriculum for educational improvement to occur. A fourth is that the most important aspects of curricula consist of words on paper, rather than actions in classrooms. Such over-simplifications endanger not only children's but also teachers' learning, especially if they focus teacher attention on the supposedly standardised and theoretical curriculum, rather than on the local and actual curriculum: the curriculum which is daily negotiated teacher to child and comes to life in classrooms. The construction of the teacher in this book suggests that such local re-negotiations of national curricula are not only essential, but unavoidable. It also argues that, if teachers are self-confident and well-supported, such negotiations can synthesise central curricula designed in legislation, with local curricula built in practice.

A further disjunction between curriculum-as-theory and curriculum-as-practice arises from the term 'history's' long-established and diverse meanings. The word can refer to a highly intellectual and specialised discipline. It can also mean a 'subject' young children are taught in schools, often by adults with little or no formal historical training. School history in this light can seem forever to be chasing an academic tail of supposed subject purity, one it is doomed never to catch. It is equally respectable for teachers to consider 'history' from the opposite direction: to demand first what the subject can offer to the learner and the curriculum, in an interdisciplinary manner, rather than what the learner can offer to the subject. If such a question can be convincingly answered by teachers then the history curriculum, locally negotiated with learners in classrooms up and down the country, seems more likely to embody some of the classic reasons commonly supposed for studying history; and less in danger of pallid regurgitation of historical content, or mindless drilling in skills. The effective use of a subject policy statement for history achieves this end. It educates the school as a whole, its learners, teachers, parents and governors, not just into *what* history is being learnt but *why* it is worth learning in the first place (see Chapters 5 and 8 in particular for documents discussing the value of learning history).

Addressing such important questions entails teachers navigating history curricula between 'inter-disciplinary and subject specific' ends; juggling the teaching of knowledge about President John F. Kennedy, for instance, with how to extract that knowledge from sources such as films, books and the Internet. It also suggests that history curricula need to teach children how to 'view history as a social activity' rather than 'one pursued only in school'. History as practised in universities, the media, heritage bodies and museums, tourism agencies and the public services; history as applied by lawyers, architects, doctors, builders and vicars is a social, as well as an intellectual practice. This practice demands personal skills (e.g. analytic thinking, imagination, clear communication, team work) cutting across intellectual disciplines (e.g. literature, statistics, archae-ology, design) deployed through specialist knowledge (e.g. historical concepts, terms, sources). History is not 'pure' history even when practised by people who are pure 'historians' and have the paycheque to prove it. Additionally, most professional historians are skilled in analysing diverse facets of historical evidence: visual and architectural, political and social, public and personal for instance, as well as written and documentary. School history can reflect this diversity of skills by considering whether it should 'advance multimedia or only written literacy skills'. The various national history curricula in England have consistently advocated such an approach, by stipulating that the history curriculum should teach children how to analyse evidence from a range of media: photos, buildings and music as well as books and documents (see DfEE 1999a). Such critical reading skills are also taught by subjects such as English, geography and citizenship; yet the curriculum as a whole, or in history, does not exist merely to service skills in isolation. The reason history is worth studying, worth spending millions of mental hours and public pounds upon in schools, is that thinking about history helps learners to question and construct values. A school's claimed overall aims, for instance to 'foster independent learning' or 'value people equally' can often be found in a brochure, mission statement or motto on a wall: historical sources of one kind. Its *actual* values can be seen in that school's interactions with people, at grassroots level, and may tell a different story: an historical source of another kind. Where education is effective, there is a good chance that these different sources have been reconciled.

For instance, how does a school demonstrate to learners that it values independent learning in its history curriculum? In what ways could it prove that it actively works for equal opportunities during its teaching of the history curriculum? History exists not just as a dead record of a distant past, but as a way of thinking leading to a prompting, questioning appraisal of the local and the present. Its value in the curriculum therefore partly rests upon teachers' planning how to use history to 'open adult values to scrutiny' rather than merely 'promoting acceptance' of a prevailing view. This includes monitoring the national curriculum in history against the school's own local aims. History's immediate processes, of telling stories and asking questions through evidence, can also lead teachers and children into a connected question. How do curricula 'reveal or obscure the grounds for history's claims to value?' In other words and even though history's immediate place in the national curriculum seems assured, as teachers we should re-view the subject afresh and through learners' eyes. Why should a child bother to learn about all these past centuries when she is only 7, 11 or 14 years old? Does this history curriculum she is experiencing explain why history is worth studying, as well as tell interesting stories about Anglo-Saxons or World War II? This entails teaching the subject not as though it were a taken-for-granted, unthinking and unchanging aspect of school life, secure for ever in its two or three lessons a week; but as only one cultural option amongst many open to young learners, both through the formal channels of school and the varied, often more alluring informal channels of play, friendship, home and media.

Policy and Politics in the History Curriculum

At the level of rhetoric, recent and current English governments seem keen to appear supportive of history in schools. The 1997 New Labour government set out its professed attitudes to education soon after taking office, declaring in its first education legislation that 'A good education provides access to this country's rich and diverse culture, to its history and to an understanding of its place in the world. It offers opportunities to gain insight into the best that has been thought and said and done' (DfEE 1997 p. 9). Theoretically, such views were carried forward into the curriculum review that took place in 1998–9. QCA, the government department responsible for the curriculum, identified at the start of that review 'two broad categories of aims which schools seek to achieve through the curriculum', these being 'opportunities for all pupils to learn and to achieve' and 'to prepare all pupils for the opportunities, responsbilities and experiences of life' (QCA 1998 pp. 4–5). Both categories could apply to studying history, as transmission of culture and the development of personal skills. For instance QCA outlined how:

> The school curriculum should contribute to the development of pupils' sense of identify through knowlede and understanding of their spiritual, moral, social and cultural heritages and of the local, national, European and international dimensions . . . It should pass on the enduring values of society . . . It should develop [pupils'] knowledge and understanding of different beliefs and cultures.
>
> (ibid. p. 5)

At one level, it seems that official support is solid for the teaching and learning of history. At another, such statements are supportive for subject leaders in the task of developing and promoting the discipline in schools. For QCA also admitted that 'these aims are not in themselves part of the statutory curriculum for schools,' imagining instead that 'they provide an essential context within which . . . schools will develop their own curriculum.' (ibid. p. 4) The government department managing curriculum envisages the curriculum review process as only half finished, when conceived of as merely a national process. Creative and interpretive work remains to be done locally, by schools, to embody 'aims' into effective and grassroot policies and pedagogies.

History subject leaders can play a prominent role in achieving this, if they can secure the support of their school's senior management team and the attention of colleagues. This is an enormous 'if'. Multiple demands still press on primary and secondary schools through continuing national initiatives on, for instance, literacy, numeracy, ICT, PSHE and citizenship. All curriculum subjects harbour similar ambitions and needs. It therefore seems unrealistic to expect that QCA's envisaged 'local curriculum development for history' will receive widespread official support in schools, if attempted in isolation. The demands of the curriculum are too complex, and the available staff time too short. Rather, as teachers of subjects such as history we need to be agile in our strategies. Rich opportunities exist to synthesise history as a discipline with curricular initiatives promoting, for instance, literacy (e.g. Bage 1999a; Counsell 1997), ICT (e.g. Walsh 1998), citizenship (e.g. Wrenn 1999) or thinking skills (e.g. Fisher 1999).

Such interdisciplinary thinking fits with the curriculum aims identified by English government policy just quoted, as well as with aims for 'learning across the curriculum' promoted in the English national curriculum itself (DfEE 1999b pp. 19–23). Cosmetically at least this clears the path for local curriculum developers to harmonise history's aims, with schools' aims, with overall national curriculum aims. Unfortunately, educational life is not quite that simple. For nestling between these various aims are located the details of national curriculum history. Framed by idealistic, lofty peaks lies the actual landscape through which teachers and children have to travel, a journey through which they hope to arrive at these aims. It is by taking this journey, a pedagogical journey, that educators transform words on curriculum pages, into individual children's learning in classrooms.

In a rational imagination this educational landscape is lovingly cultivated; and although winding roads twist through the rich towns and fertile fields, the surrounding peaks and mountains offer landmarks to ensure that nobody becomes lost. The local material for this key stage, or that subject, is carefully piloted, evaluated, selected and presented. These materials support the stated aims of the national curriculum, link with other subjects and enable schools to use a discipline like history to meet and develop their own aims.

Unfortunately, history teaches us that our world is not this rational place. The material details of national curriculum history fit ill with some of the national curriculum's stated aims. Theoretically, this latter should 'equip pupils with the essential learning skills of literacy, numeracy and information and communication technology' (DfEE 1999b p. 11). Yet the overall subject-by-subject structure of the English national curriculum was designed long before the birth of national numeracy and literacy strategies, the national grid for learning or the advent of 'citizenship'; and the content of a subject such as history remains unchanged and conservative despite, or perhaps because of, the educational maelstrom that has whirled around it.

For example the national curriculum in history demands that 7 to 11 year olds study Tudor period 'significant events and individuals, including monarchs'

(DfEE 1999a p. 18); but not that children learn about the history of education itself, a process which dominates so much of their own, daily lives. School curricula should, we are told 'promote pupils' self-esteem and emotional well-being' (DfEE 1999b p. 11); yet in the English KS3 national curriculum in history there is no possibility of studying young people in the past as a distinctive theme and no mention of the possibility or importance of studying personal relationships and the affective domain in history. According to the national curriculum's overall rationale, school curricula should contribute to pupils' 'knowledge and understanding of . . . European, Commonwealth and global dimensions' (ibid.); yet if pupils follow the national curriculum, the majority renounce history at 14 having glimpsed Ancient Greece and probably Egypt in the Primary school and perhaps the French Revolution, some native American Indians and a World War at secondary school. The English government claims to believe that school curricula should develop 'respect for the environments in which [students] live and secure their commitment to sustainable development' (ibid.); yet it is highly likely that children will pass through compulsory history education between the ages of 4 and 14 without ever studying hunting and gathering societies, the early development of agriculture, the processes of archaeology or the importance of climate in history.

Although we could continue with this list of contradictions, we should stop for perhaps three reasons. The first is that the main point has been made. The national curriculum is a hotch-potch affair of often conflicting aims and content, desperately needing more teacher-translation, not less. The second is that many effective teachers and schools have overcome these inherent problems; see, for instance, any recent issue of the Historical Association's *Teaching History* or *Primary History*, or peruse the excellent range of English Heritage magazines, booklets and videos. The third is that, like it or not, national curricula are here to stay as a global phenomenon. The current English example may not be the worst of this bunch and has merits as well as deficits. Perhaps its most important strength is that since 1990-91, teachers in England have been working within a continuous framework, if sometimes adapted and changed through practice. Such continuity has enabled them in some cases to develop an extensive toolkit of classroom materials and teaching ideas with which to build the history curriculum on the ground. Continuity, even within flawed or incomplete overall curricular designs, has enabled practical improvements in history, especially where educators have been able to accumulate expertise and confidence. It has also helped build a bank of expertise in some local and national advisory services, upon which schools can draw to support new or changing staff. Where this is not the case, where schools have a high staff turnover, challenging social circumstances and a declining quality or level of LEA support, the benefits of such continuity in the national curriculum are least likely to apply. It is areas such as this which are most likely to become 'Education Action Zones' and where, appropriately, the national curriculum can be suspended.

In other words and in practice, this national curriculum is not 'national' at all. Where it is patently not working, it can be disapplied. Where it still holds sway its 'subjects' such as history neither uniformly conform with what the government claims are the overall aims of school curricula; nor can they be simply 'taught' without considerable local mediation by teachers. Indeed this option is built into the 2000 version of the English history national curriculum, which entwines 'local history' into the programme of study in creative ways.

If this seems a perplexing state of current affairs, perhaps history can explain them? A fuller history of the history national curriculum has been so brilliantly pursued elsewhere (e.g. Phillips 1998) that I shall not offer a further one. What can be attempted is a sketch of four key and sometimes contradictory themes in this history, which you as reader might find useful for plotting your personal course through history education.

Some Themes in Recent History Education

You might consider as you read which of these themes have been echoed in your personal or professional experience. Perhaps even more importantly, reflect upon whether and how these different threads might be reconciled. For the argument will be made in the next section that teachers' 'critical mediation' of national curricula is essential to its success. This is not just because constructivist theory teaches that individual knowing matters most, nor only because fine teaching implies creativity and confidence. It is also because the English 2000 national curriculum is not the well-balanced, rational and thoughtful beast that its image-makers like to project. In common with many documents produced by official committees, what lies under the gloss is more of a muddle than most governments want us to know.

Theme 1   *History in Education is Generally Perceived as 'in Danger'*

Phillips' own recent book ended with the suggestion that, due to changes in the national curriculum, history might be 'once more in danger' (1998 p. 135). This theme had been consistent throughout the curriculum debate of the previous thirty years (ibid. p. 15) although it gave rise to two broadly distinctive approaches. The first was that the danger lay more in conservative curricula and pedagogies, which needed reform if history was to survive as a lively and relevant discipline, attractive to young people. This thinking led to 1970s and 1980s innovations such as the Humanities Curriculum Project and the Schools History Project (e.g. Farmer and Knight 1995 Chapter 1; Hadyn, Arthur and Hunt 1997 Chapter 2); to a 'new history' emphasising skills and ideas over content and eventually, to the incorporation of 'skills, knowledge and understanding' articulated by the current history national curriculum (DfEE 1999a). In contrast the second approach saw history as endangered not by the prevalence of educational tradition but by its scarcity. According to this argument, the pre-national curriculum innovations designed to 'save' history were, in reality, destroying its coherence and undermining the narrative traditions of well-established topics, texts and teaching styles. Such thinking gave rise throughout the 1990s to a host of Conservative pressure groups, politicians and education secretaries wishing to pose as protectors of 'traditional' history; and especially of chronological, British and narrative aspects of the same. A single instance will suffice here as an example of a well-documented trend (e.g. Crawford 1995; McKiernan 1993; Phillips 1998):

> John Patten, the education secretary, is proposing a new legal requirement that infant children aged five to seven should be taught specific facts about British history . . . The change will be seen as a further move to tilt the balance in the curriculum towards British history for children of all ages.
> (*Sunday Times* 1 May 1994 'Britain put at history's heart')

Such thinking exercised significant influence over the choice of content articulated by the first and second English national history curricula. This influence, if government-influenced media reports were to be believed, extended to the third and current attempt.

> The eleventh hour reinstatement of classic writers and the addition of early British history to the compulsory national curriculum has been hailed as a victory for parents by traditionalists . . . In a last-minute hardening of the Government line, Education Secretary David Blunkett . . . made the study of the Romans, Anglo-Saxons and Vikings and Tudors compulsory for junior pupils for the first time.
> (*TES* 10 September 1999 'Ministers revert to literary tradition')

The question remains open as to whether the rather ill-fitting compromise between these two constructed 'dangers' renders educational history sufficiently robust to prosper in the face of newer and perhaps greater threats. Technological advances, media revolutions, cultural globalisation, economic consumerism, social restructuring, political reform and ethnic change may all offer 'history' greater opportunities, or threats, than the previously rather narrow squabbles over the English national curriculum may suggest.

Theme 2   *National Curriculum History has been Heavily Influenced by 'New Right' and 'Cultural Restorationist' Thinking*

The cramped nature of much recent discussion of the history curriculum perhaps reflects that much debate over national curriculum history was, and still is, being played out on ground chosen by the 'new right'. Crawford (1995) persuasively argued that in the early 1990s this grouping promulgated 'moral panics' to steer history policy making towards a conservative agenda. This was achieved by playing on fears of English national decline, splintering British identity and the supposed liberal extremism of some politically untrustworthy educators. Ball argued similarly that conservative thinking was dominated by a 'cultural restorationist image of the Victorian schoolroom' and that:

> The most visible aspect of the Conservative government's educational reforms is the development and installation of the National Curriculum.

Not since the nineteenth century Revised Codes has a UK government attempted to assert direct control over the school curriculum.

(1994 p. 33)

Through a national curriculum in history, ran Ball's argument, Conservative propaganda envisaged that 'The blood, struggle, pain and mess of history is reworked into a litany of glories and victories, a retrospective and sentimental adjustment of the actual' (ibid. p. 39). Another analyst traced changes in the particulars of the first history national curriculum to these conservative ideological influences, asserting that the results 'enabled *traditional* history teachers to teach traditional history' (McKiernan 1993 p. 50). Although such a thesis has convincing aspects, it also has two major weaknesses. Firstly it tends to ignore some contradictory evidence from the three English national curricula themselves of 1991, 1995 and 2000; evidence from within the very educational artefacts supposed to have been so shaped by these conservative forces. For instance teaching history now should involve teaching 'interpretations', referring to 'evidence' and examining different 'perspectives', thanks to national curricula. Secondly, such a theoretical thesis ignores the ability and willingness of practitioners to interpret, often liberally, the theoretical dictats which may be imposed by centralist governments, but cannot be practised by them. This book encourages practitioners along such an interpretative path and offers tools to assist on the journey.

Equally, it would be naive to ignore evidence of the power that broadly conservative ideologies continue to wield over history curriculum-making. The following two quotations stem from the 1999 debate about changes to the English national curriculum in history. Both derive from the same article and could, in effect, have come from the same politician. In reality, one was the (then) Tory and Opposition spokeswoman speaking, Teresa May. The other was the (then) New Labour education minister, Estelle Morris. Can you as reader spot which was which, and who was who?

Our priority for the national curriculum is to ensure that important key events and historical figures and developments in British history will be retained. This will ensure that pupils learn the richness of British history.

Teaching our children the history of our country is a very important part of education. It gives schoolchildren a sense of national identity and of what has made this country what it is today.

(*The Guardian* 5 August 1999 'Tories protest at history shift')

The refusal to acknowledge any difference in approach to such fine-detailed curricular matters speaks volumes of how political sensitivities and insecurities about 'national identity' can build to a ridiculous pitch when 'educational history' is in the public eye.

The 'New Labour' statement was actually the first quoted . . .

Theme 3   National Curriculum History is Inherently 'Racist and Sexist'

The assertion that national curriculum history is inherently racist and sexist sits comfortably with analyses examined previously. Gillborn saw clear evidence of how 'The debates surrounding the 1993 Education Act provide a clear example of how the new racism has operated through cultural restorationism in education . . . this discourse constructs ethnic minority communities as outsiders . . . who present a direct challenge to 'our' traditions and faith' (1997 pp. 352–3). Asserting the importance of a national curriculum in history, particularly one dominated by Anglo-centric choices of content, is by this logic a small cog in a large and deliberate machine. Such arguments rest upon empirics as well as theorising. Weiner for instance analysed the first national curriculum to argue that:

> . . . of the thirty-one named individuals in the core course, only two are women and all are Europeans. Additionally, of the ninety-three named individuals who may be studied in the optional units, only nine are women and a further two (males) originate from outside Europe.
>
> (1993 p. 92)

Such criticisms persist to the present. The Historical Association's response to preliminary proposals in 1999 for revising the national curriculum saw imbalance in its examples of important events and personalities 'too many relate to white, Anglo-centric male history' (Lomas 1999 p. 6). An earlier and private response supplied to QCA was more forthright: 'There are missed opportunities to develop multicultural understanding . . . the proposals here seem to reinforce stereotyping rather than breaking down barriers. Although the Historical Association welcomes the stress on linking Britain and the wider world, this itelf does not guarantee an improvement in multicultural understanding' (HA 1999 p. 1). The curricular inertia so identified by the Historical Association and many others came just months after the Macpherson report starkly catalogued the brutal racism surrounding Stephen Lawrence's murder in 1993. This report made the well-publicised recommendation that 'consideration be given to amendment of the National Curriculum aimed at valuing cultural diversity and preventing racism, in order better to reflect the needs of a diverse society' (Macpherson 1999 p. 334). Such a sentiment made little impact in the case of history in the national curriculum.

Theme 4   National Curriculum History Extends 'Entitlement' in History

In apparent contrast to some of the arguments mustered under theme 3, commentators have also interpreted the national curriculum as a chance to promote comprehensive and inclusive views of British history. The argument about comprehensive access is convincing. Before 1991 the provision for subjects such as history was patchy, particularly in primary schools (e.g. DES 1989) and depended much upon the individual whims of teachers even in secondary schools (e.g. Barnes 1976; Hull 1986). According to a classically Conservative source the

1991 'original national curriculum was so prescriptive' in order to solve such perceived problems. This prescriptive curriculum 'was intended to guarantee a minimum entitlement to all children, no matter which kind of school they attended' (*The Daily Telegraph* 5 August 1999 'Why history is not what it used to be'). Despite changes since that 1991 introduction, all children currently following the English national curriculum still have to study history up to the age of 14. Through national legislation the discipline secured a curricular toehold, exposing all children to a basic curriculum minimum of history. This 'entitlement' argument has been extended by some educators, through detailed and often grounded interpretations of national curriculum content. Claire (1996), Hazareesingh (1994) and Pankhania (1994), for instance, painstakingly mediated the bulk of national history curriculum content into creative, inventive and multicultural forms. Their aim was to support curriculum diversification through developing multicultural histories within the 'national' curriculum. Although such opportunities persist into the current history curriculum the essentially conservative, subject-based structure into which it fits tests the notion of 'entitlement', especially 'multicultural entitlement', to its limit. For the English national curriculum in history was founded upon the idea that its introduction could reinforce a sense of British national identity (Bage 1998), itself associated with a raft of other cultural values:

> After the union of England with Scotland which formed Britain in 1707, we grew used to thinking of Britain as a righteous, Christian country . . . as the most civilised of nations, superior not only to other European countries, but also to the Indians and Africans . . . This traditional nationalism is . . . in terminal recession . . . Our traditional attachment to British national values . . . is crumbling with the years.
>
> (White 1997 pp. 19–20)

Fearful of being seen to contribute to this supposed decline, governments have consistently used the history curriculum to bolster a supposed, but increasingly mythic Britishness. They have also under-valued a moral imperative implied by the McPherson (1999) report just alluded to: namely, that a radical, multi-cultural and English, not necessarily British, reconstruction of school history might be necessary, if racism is to be tackled and English national identity clarified. Such a reconstruction could benefit English white, working class youth, if recent empirical research into racism in Greenwich is to be believed, as well as English children from ethnic minority backgrounds:

> White pupils, to some extent, seem like cultural ghosts, haunting as mere absences the richly decorated corridors of multicultural society. And when they attempt to turn to the symbols and emblems of 'their' cultural identity, they find either very little that fits their needs or, in the case of the Union Jack, that the emblem itself is already a contested battle-ground.
>
> (Hewitt 1996 p. 40)

Teachers and the History Curriculum

Teachers respond to curricula, especially centrally imposed curricula, in different but predictable ways. Pollard et al (1994), in their longitudinal study of how a representative group of eighty-eight KS1 teachers responded to the first national curriculum in England, tested and adapted an existing conceptual framework analysing change. Their subsequent research identified the following types of response to national curricula:

Compliance: acceptance of the imposed changes and adjustment of teachers' professional ideology accordingly, so that greater central control is perceived as acceptable, or even desirable.

Incorporation: appearing to accept the imposed changes but incorporating them into existing modes of working, so that existing methods are adapted rather than changed and the effect of change is considerably different from that intended.

Mediation: taking active control of the changes and responding to them in a creative, but possibly selective way.

Retreatism: submission to the imposed changes without any change in professional ideology, leading to deep-seated feelings of resentment, demoralization and alienation.

Resistance: resistance to the imposed changes in the hope that the sanctions available to enforce them will not be sufficiently powerful to make this impossible.

Pollard et al. (1994) p. 100

One reason for including this model here is that, as a reader, you may recognise your own responses to curriculum on such a continuum. Another is to argue that 'mediation', understood as critical mediation, is the most constructive attitude for teachers to adopt to curricula. This is not only for ideological reasons, but also for pragmatic ones: 'critical mediation' stands a better chance than the others of improving teaching and learning. This did not always happen in the early stages of the English national curriculum in history. Sometimes the history community was so flattered at history's curricular inclusion that national curriculum structures were viewed through rosy lenses: 'compliance' or 'incorporation' prevailed. Equally, teachers struggling with multiple change could feel so swamped that 'retreatism' or 'resistance' appeared (Phillips 1998). 'Critical mediation' took time to surface, especially mediation derived from practice as well as theory. Now that the English national curriculum in history has been in existence for a decade and more, albeit with some changes, critical mediation may become more common. Such critical mediation can happen more easily if as teachers we have access to the tools and time with which to open and rearrange the curriculum box for ourselves. This book is written to assist that mission. It takes its place alongside many others offering related answers to a fundamental and always useful critically mediating question: what is history for?

Cooper (1995a) for instance, argues from theory and practice how history as ideas and activities enriches an early years curriculum. The passing of time is seen as central to the experience of young children's lives and the questions 'what is it like to be someone else?' and 'how do I know it is true?' crucial to the developing intellectual independence of 4–7 year olds. Her work sketches how experiencing history through 'stories, play-reading, writing, talking, drawing and model-making' are 'central to social, emotional and cognitive growth' in this age range (ibid. p. 4). Dewey, some century earlier, captured and reinforced a similar argument: that a rigid distinction between planning history pedagogy and planning history curriculum was dangerous in the primary years.

> If the aim of historical instruction is to enable the child to appreciate the values of social life, to see in imagination the forces which favour and let men's effective co-operation with one another, to understand the sorts of character that help on and that hold back, the essential thing in its presentation is to make it moving, dynamic. History must be presented not as an accumulation of results or effects, but as a forceful, acting thing. The motives – that is, the motors, must stand out. To study history is not to amass information, but to use information in constructing a vivid picture of how and why men did thus and so, achieved their successes and came to their failures.
>
> (Findlay, ed. n.d. p. 96)

Given such a starting point it is impossible simply to take any theoretical curriculum shell and 'apply' it in classrooms to 'cover' pre-defined historical content or learning objectives. Instead, the mobile nature of young children's thinking is presumed to mirror the mobility in the human condition, which history does so much to describe. Blyth (1994 p. 154) bridges the gap between Dewey and Cooper, early and primary years, with a prescient summary:

> The basic problem in primary history is how to combine development in children's thinking with the sweep of history itself. Inevitably there must be selection of content and . . . that selection involves bias of some kind, for neither timetables nor children's minds are infinite in capacity.

He continues the argument to offer guidelines for the development of the historical perspective in the primary curriculum. This framework, when laid alongside the national curriculum, helps any 'critical mediator' of curricula in history, by highlighting the importance of managing, but moving beyond, particular cognitive objectives:

- young children should have an idea of the major epochs of Western history combined with a firm recognition that there are other histories too, of other continents;

- they should realise that real adult people with great achievements lived in the past;
- that there can be great stimulus and pleasure in learning about the past;
- that there are no simple right/wrong answers about the past;
- that the historical perspective should always be considered when looking at problems in the present.

(ibid.)

Such a broader view was articulated in early government documents introducing the national curriculum in history (e.g. DES 1990). Unfortunately at that stage many teachers were neither given, nor took the time, to plan and monitor how such broader aims of history as a subject could be tested against the more specific content and objectives with which the national curriculum seemed so concerned: against 'Victorian Britain' or 'handling sources', for instance. It is such specificities, such 'skills' and 'studies' (DfEE 1999a), such slabs of content and slices of process, which still dominate so much professional practice and public debate. In contrast, such big ideas of educational history as 'helping to give pupils a sense of identity' for instance, or 'contributing to pupils' knowledge and understanding of other countries and cultures in the modern world' (DES 1990a p. 1) are commonly treated as buried foundations, rather than architectural features letting in light and air. Why? Perhaps because it is easy to assume as a teacher, when under pressure to cover the curriculum, that such fundamental aims can be activated simply through children experiencing say a 'period of local history' or 'native American peoples'. We often therefore trip into the trap of over-teaching prescribed content and skills, rather than exploring the discipline's fundamental aims. This is a huge mistake. If history is to prosper in schools 'History teachers need to be able to articulate a convincing case for the subject's place in the school curriculum, to parents, pupils and other teachers' (Hadyn, Arthur and Hunt 1997 p. 27). Such a case cannot rest on the lame justification 'we are doing this because it is in the national curriculum – or exam syllabus'.

Some politicians understand this well, as this prominent and radical 1980s figure exemplified: 'History, properly taught, justifies its place in the school curriculum by what it does to prepare all pupils for the responsibility of citizenship as well as the demands of employment and the opportunities of leisure' (Joseph 1984). The current national curriculum in history even attempts to integrate such thinking into teachers' practices, rather than merely into curriculum theorising, by heading its few pages with a paragraph outlining 'The distinctive contribution of history to the school curriculum' (ibid. p. 132). If this opening statement is given the weight and attention it deserves, critical and questioning mediation of what follows is axiomatic. If history's 'distinctive contribution' is ignored the national curriculum in history, for all its identification of apparently process-based objectives, can again be moulded into a parade of disconnected exercises and texts: appealing to hard-pressed teachers and profit-hungry publishers but of increasing puzzlement, even irrelevance, to large numbers of students. Learners, especially as they pass into secondary education, soon realise that life in and beyond school may diverge dramatically.

If teachers are unable to turn curricula into materials that span this divergence, and create lessons making history feel like a once lived and human experience, the curriculum and the discipline desiccate into dull, empty shells. For despite the fact that by definition, readers of this book will have experience and interest in history education, we all know too that:

> Life outside school does not come packaged in the conceptually tidy tasks that the structure of a discipline represents; hence the focus on that structure can increase the isolation of the disciplines and may, in fact, diminish rather than increase the student's ability to transfer what he or she has learned.

> (Eisner 1994 p. 84)

How the curriculum copes with this, how the curriculum itself critically mediates between the competing realities of the society it exists in, and the sometimes contradictory or unrealistic aims set for it, is an acid test of the curriculum's worth. History as a discipline has a special place in this process, for it claims to be teaching students how to understand the very cycles of change, continuity and power of which the curriculum itself is a product. The extent to which that product has been designed following the principles which it espouses, such as 'reason', 'democracy' or 'equal opportunities', has already been thrown into doubt. It is therefore doubly important that us teachers, whose task it is to make the curriculum work, can see clearly a national curriculum's shortcomings: for it is we who must move most swiftly to improve it through our practice.

4   Community History

History isn't what happened. History is just what historians tell us . . . And we, the readers of history, the sufferers from history, we scan the pattern for hopeful conclusions, for the way ahead . . . The history of the world? Just voices echoing in the dark; images that burn for a few centuries and then fade; stories, old stories that sometimes seem to overlap . . .

(Barnes 1989 p. 242)

Mapping the Questions

Underlying Questions About How Communities:

View schools or central government as key controllers of the curriculum?	*Governance Issues*
Promote singular or multicultural histories in schools?	*Issues of Diversity*
Interact with their history through popular as well as specialist media?	*Media Issues*
Are comprehensive or selective in their aspirations for history?	*Values-led Issues*
Are active or passive in pursuit of their own histories?	*Democratic Issues*
Understand history as school work or lifelong knowledge?	*Cognitive Issues*
Perceive historical knowledge as made individually or collectively?	*Social Issues*

This book asks you as a reader to place yourself on a map of educational history. It also reflects upon how, as you and I plot individual routes through history's educational terrain, we steer our journeys. If practising as teachers we frequently negotiate the local landscapes of classrooms, learning and teaching, some important features of which were discussed in Chapters 1 and 2. These local immediacies and contexts are also overlaid by the national themes of Chapter 3; for 'the curriculum', especially 'the national curriculum', has come to dominate educational history in England as elsewhere. Chapter 4 concludes this section of the book by examining how these dimensions of history learning, teaching and curricula relate to communities. For ultimately it is to communities that educators are answerable and it is from communities that schools are funded, staffed and controlled.

An axis in this relationship is the extent to which communities 'view schools or central government as key controllers of the curriculum'. Reading 1990s sources for recent English educational history, such as policy documents or national newspapers, might suggest an intense communal yearning for governments to control history curricula and so reinforce national identity (e.g. Phillips 1998). Local realities were perhaps more complex: the letters' page of 1990s local newspapers, or the minutes of school governors' and parents' meetings, rarely bulged with as much historical dispute as conservative newspapers. Nevertheless, parents of school-aged children do seem to care deeply about individual children's history learning. A decade into the national curriculum, the author helped research and write a study of KS2 history teaching and learning in ten primary schools from inner-city, urban, suburban and rural England (Bage, Grisdale and Lister 1999). This examined the educational impact of the Ancient Greeks and Romans in particular, but also surveyed the broader views of parents or guardians about the history their children were learning. Just over a third of parents replied to a questionnaire (227) and in only a tiny proportion were negative values about history expressed. History was a valued curriculum element, ranked fifth 'in importance' out of eleven subject areas behind English, maths, science and information technology. History was esteemed by such parents because, as explained in their own words below, many thought studying history helped their children understand and identify with society: not because, by doing it, their children helped preserve the nation.

History gives a sense of identity and continuity.

(Essex parent)

Only by understanding what has gone before can children really establish their own identity and place within society.

(Lancashire parent)

It widens their knowledge and helps them evaluate that things change and progress. My eldest child, who is 10, is very interested in history and has actually told me things that I never knew.

(London parent)

Barely a handful of the 155 responses to the open-ended question 'do you see any gains or benefits your child makes from learning history?' used the media language of 'British' or 'English' identity crisis. This survey therefore threw light on the question of whether communities perceived 'historical knowledge as made individually or collectively?' These parents nearly all saw individual understanding of history as a way to start developing collective identity, rather than the other way around. Parents may 'like' a national curriculum: but only if their particular children have been helped to make something of it, via the mediation of pedagogy. National curricula rely upon such mediation because, being national and of necessity simple, they can easily and clumsily overgeneralise. For instance, it was not only conservative journalists who were concerned about whether 1990s schools and history curricula reflected modern English identities:

Black youth of African or Afro-Caribbean descent born in Britain, or who have grown up here, have a major identity crisis . . .The second and third generations are being deprived, through serious omissions and lack of acknowledgement, of a sense of continuity and confidence about the contributions that Black people have made to British history.

(Garrison 1994 p. 239)

In similar vein practising teachers have doubted the collective thrust of the national curriculum, in this case exploring dilemmas surrounding an historical visit to a medieval castle by an ethnically mixed class:

I was conscious that when the children are asked to go back in time, only the ones with white parents would imagine that it was their own great, great grandparents that they might encounter. For the Asian ones . . . it's a different exercise . . . Would the Anglo school children in rural Nottinghamshire be asked to fly back in time, ever, to a place where everyone looked different and they had no relatives?

(Griffiths 1995 p. 102)

Returning to underlying questions sketched in our map, to what extent should history curricula 'promote singular or multicultural histories in schools?' A national curriculum may secure a minimum entitlement to diversity but can just as easily maximise exclusion from it. As this reviewer of 2000 English national curriculum history argued 'the content of the proposed 'new' history curriculum fails to recognise the cosmopolitan nation that Britain is today' (Grosvenor 1999 pp. 39–40).

Community and teacher-mediation of such curricula is essential. Grosvenor went on to argue that 'it is teachers who make the difference not centrally directed structures' (ibid. p. 40), bringing us on our map to a related question: whether communities 'are comprehensive or selective in their aspirations for history?' An important supposed benefit of national curricula is that they offer everybody 'entitlement' to a minimal understanding of community history. An equally important problem arises, in our multicultural and socially diverse modern England, when all children are unselectively offered the same history: a singular and national 'community's history' rather than plural, regional or local 'community histories'. In this case as teachers we should perhaps act as representatives not so much of central government to the local community, as of the local community to central government. Our role then is not to impose a government-approved version of national history upon all English communities and children; but to select the content from within and beyond the nationally-agreed framework which most benefits our local community and children. Curricula decided by national means could then openly be adapted for local communities' use; the 'comprehensive' element lying more in common access to challenging, thought-provoking historical thinking, less in a supposedly uniform cultural heritage.

From this idea flow others. If as teachers we genuinely desired schools and history to matter to our children and local community, we would monitor whether communities themselves 'are active or passive in pursuit of their own histories'. We would flavour the national curriculum with knowledge of our local community's histories from long-term residents, local historians and storytellers, libraries and record offices, guardians of the built and natural environments, the local media and community figures such as councillors, religious leaders or business people. Local perspectives could then populate and re-interpret national history, as the last section of this chapter discusses, secure that the national curriculum stipulated this anyway.

As community-led historians we and our children would actively engage with communities' popular histories. Some histories would be found in local media such as newspapers and museums, and in individual stories or memories. Others would be represented in national media especially television, film, newspapers and websites. Even though such populist histories seem crude to some academic historical specialists, they are educationally and socially inescapable. *Educationally* because including populist history in school history is the lifeblood of historical interpretations and evidence. It models how history is constructed and communicated in most people's worlds, and is an essential element of the English national curriculum history requirements, to study 'historical interpretation' (DfEE 1999a pp. 16-20). *Socially* because starting from populist as well as specialist history helps answer a fundamental question, asked by any well-taught student:

Student Why am I learning all this old stuff?
Teacher Because when you look at the telly and newspapers, old stuff is most of what's there.

In modern England communities 'interact with their history through popular as well as specialist media' as television schedules show and academics have argued (e.g. Lowenthal 1998; Samuel 1994). Fine teachers exploit this and teach history through more than textbooks, lessons and classrooms. Such variegated practice brings us to the final underlying question from our map: the extent to which communities 'understand history as school work or lifelong knowledge?' As a reader both may be reflected in your own life experience, as they are in mine. For instance I have developed a lifelong love of history; yet the chasm yawns between my schoolchild experiences of history and my feelings about history now. Local history, spoken history, history stories, visual histories, landscape history, living history: these are the things I enjoy most as a 43 year old. As a 10 year old I experienced none of them at primary school, nor was to do so in secondary or even university history education. Instead, my memories of history at secondary school are dominated by the paraphernalia of work: tasks, goals, lists, tests, exams, essays, grades, assessments, competition and so on. Since small children grow into job-seeking adults, secondary curricula need 'work'. Equally, we can hope that English children growing up in the twenty-first century will develop not just into 'workers' but into creative, sociable, balanced, challenging, moral and leisure-loving adults, capable of seizing the numerous cultural opportunities that sophisticated technologies and economies can provide. Creating such futures is part of what education is about: 'Statements of aims and objectives . . . refer forward in time . . . futures are already present, already there in present-day teaching and learning' (Beare and Slaughter 1993 p. 102). The English national curriculum sets itself the task of staying flexible for the future and demands that teachers be even more so:

> The curriculum itself cannot remain static . . . Teachers individually and collectively, have to reappraise their teaching in response to the changing needs of their pupils and the impact of economic, social and cultural change. Education only flourishes if it successfully adapts to the demands and needs of the time.
>
> (DfEE 1999c p. 13)

Nevertheless, the 2000 national curriculum has distinctively retrospective traits (Alexander 1984, 1997), centred on the assumption that communities value literacy, numeracy and science above all. Such an assumption is disputed, even within official curriculum thinking. For instance in 1999 a bulky, 220 page 'expert report' was produced by the government on creativity, culture and education (DfEE 1999d). It argued that 'the existing distinction between core and foundation subjects should be removed' (p. 172) and neatly summarised how the conformist pressures of inspections, SATs, league tables and target-setting can enmesh communities and schools in a spiralling decline of curriculum:

> Some areas of achievement are tested objectively and validated externally: others are left to teacher assessment. Only the former are used in judging the effectiveness of schools, and only these are monitored. The focus of teaching narrows, and so does children's learning and achievement . . . arts and humanities . . . some forms of teaching and learning . . . and some aspects of particular subjects are neglected.
>
> (DfEE 1999d p. 109)

Meanwhile the same government department was busy producing an equally bulky document describing the 'new' national curriculum (DfEE 1999b, 1999c) embodying the very contradictions and dilemmas referred to above. This muddled approach should come as no surprise, for aspects of prevailing English educational policy uncritically incorporate ethics of business and economy, without undertaking the really hard work of thinking through whether and how these things fit together. Take for instance the historical metaphor underlying this pretty typical example of official rhetoric, arguing for 'fresh' policies in early years and primary education:

> Investment in learning in the 21st century is the equivalent of investment in the machinery and technical innovation that was essential to the first great industrial revolution. Then it was physical capital; now it is human capital. We need to build up the store of knowledge and keep abreast of rapid technological development if we are to prepare the future generation.
>
> (DfEE 1997 p. 15)

Learning is constructed as a race against time and others: conceptualised as a striving towards the economic and technical goals of profitability and efficiency, a business investment yielding an industrial return. 'History' meanwhile serves as illustrative backcloth to support a simplistic, modernist causal connection: because the eighteenth century industrial revolution is perceived as a 'good thing', it is assumed that the twenty-first century needs one too. The prevalence of such thinking forces governments into ever-more-exact measurements of changes in children's literacy and numeracy, and to ever-more-desperate, even preposterous faith in the power of this technology, or that new initiative and management device, miraculously to transform education. For the political imperative to be seen as achieving better 'school work' by 'raising standards' throughout 'the system', without questioning whether standardised systems of work suit teaching and learning communities, swamps the educational impera- tive. This is to foster not just a lifelong ability to learn, but a lifelong love of learning. History, of course, teaches the power of both; history off course achieves neither.

Historical Imagination

This chapter's final section is an attempt to keep you as reader, and myself as writer, deft on our critical feet. We shall examine the relationship between the national curriculum's claim to represent the history that communities want their children to learn, and four aspects of history which seem important in many communal activities: historical imagination, heritage, Englishness and locality. It will be argued that only the latter is explicit and consistent in national curriculum 2000; and therefore that local 'teacher mediation' of that curriculum is as important as it is inevitable.

This is not to detract from the justifiable aim of any national curriculum, to offer a vision of what history offers a community's children. For instance, the opening paragraph of the 2000 history curriculum describing 'The importance of history' appeals through motivational rhetoric in its first sentence. In similar vein to the industrial/learning metaphor just examined above, it also pays homage to utilitarian reasoning in its last sentence:

> History fires pupils' curiosity about the past . . . In history, pupils find evidence, weigh it up and reach their own conclusions. To do this they need to be able to research, sift through evidence, and argue for their point of view – skills that are prized in adult life.

> (DfEE 1999a p. 14)

Below this written statement and on the same page, an example of children's historical learning is pasted, designed to illustrate the importance of history. Unfortunately it is also inconsistent with many official messages. For readers lacking access to the text, I will describe the page and its three components. In the top left hand third, a seated schoolboy and schoolgirl are photographed scrutinising documents of some sort. In the top right hand third is the official statement on 'The importance of history', from which we have just read. Across the bottom two thirds of the whole page is transcribed an imagined letter to 'Ma and Pa', from the point of view of a 1940, evacuee child. This describes a train journey, an air raid and fellow evacuees waiting in a village hall to be chosen by host families. The writer of the letter, 'Marion', and her little sister 'Winifred', are eventually picked out by the strict 'Mrs Stick'.

I have often worked with children to support such writing, and as a teacher I would be pleased if a Y6 child in my class had produced this letter. It displays imagination, empathy and considerable skill in constructing a descriptive narrative. Yet the official summative paragraph just above it, underscoring 'The importance of history' in the national curriculum, cites none of these qualities. It only ventures as far into the affective as 'curiosity', during that brave opening sentence, before retreating through its verbs into the bland abstractions of skills-led logic. Pupils 'consider . . . develop . . . see . . . understand . . . learn . . . weigh . . . research . . . sift . . . argue' but heaven forbid: this official national curriculum history does not ask that children *imagine.* It is therefore even more surprising, on the very next page of the national curriculum, to find a quotation from Dr Christine Carpenter of the University of Cambridge, claiming that history needs to do just this. 'History is an unusual discipline. Its core is hard fact . . . At the same time you have to be deductive, perceptive and imaginative in the use of that fact' (ibid. p. 15).

The detail and content of 'official' educational history conflict with the visual and semantic rhetoric used to adorn it. They also grate against the views of history learners, from Marion in primary school through to Christine in university. For the word 'imagination' is not used at all in national curriculum history 2000, despite the fact that most practical and theoretical evidence about teaching and learning history suggests that 'imagination' is crucial to these processes. The past, by chronological definition, no longer exists as a state: it can only be reconstructed through and in the imaginations of the present.

It could be argued that teaching and learning history through 'imagination' is implied in national curriculum history's later descriptions of the knowledge, skills and understanding that 'pupils should be taught', especially in 'historical interpretation, enquiry, organisation and communication'. Nevertheless, un-helpfully and throughout the document, the educationally central processes of imagination are overlayed and obscured by technicist padding; and the term 'imagination' is omitted completely. Equivalents would be for the maths curriculum to leave out shape, or for art to eschew paint. As educators we must realise this omission, for without using and enhancing 'imagination' educational history is a senseless activity.

'Imagination' informs this discussion of 'community and history' for at least two other reasons. The first is that despite imagination's omission from the 2000 English history national curriculum, coeval English government documents created exactly the opposite impression about imagination's educational importance:

> The contribution of the humanities to creative and cultural development is not sufficiently recognised . . . Yet for all the strictness of the disciplines, that

essentially is what the humanities are. The humanities offer an under-standing and an interpretation of human behaviour. *The creative process allows for imaginative activity in making and interpreting connections. These skills can help young people to make sense of their environment and past. There is a deeply-rooted sense in which people identify 'their' culture in terms of the past and /or their surroundings.*

(DfEE 1999d p. 185 my italics)

In other words, learners use history and geography to imagine themselves into their community, to learn about affection and belonging, as well as to acquire the analytic skills of evidence and argument. Teachers 'know' this: that we must teach our children to care about their learning, their community and themselves if we are to teach them anything. Unfortunately the discourse of official curriculum seems to find it almost impossible to represent such 'care' in its content, in a subject such as history.

Heritage

A second reason for emphasising the relationship between imagination, educational history and community connects with and helps explain the first. National curriculum history may have consistently omitted explicit references to 'imagination' in a desperate attempt to distinguish itself from the very industry through which most people in industrialised nations now commonly experience their past: 'heritage'.

Heritage is not our sole link with the past. History, tradition, memory, myth, and memoir variously join us with what has passed, with forebears, with our own earlier selves. But the lure of heritage now outpaces other modes of retrieval . . . 95 per cent of existing museums postdate the Second World War . . . UNESCO protocols enthrone heritage as the sovereign core of collective identity and self-respect, a nutriment as necessary as food and drink.

(Lowenthal 1998 pp. 3–5)

By experiencing heritage through its myriad media of museums, television programmes, theme parks, publishing and retailing, the modern person is made to feel in touch with the past. This helps compensate for contemporary 'isolation and dislocation of self from family, family from neighbourhood, neighbourhood from nation . . . Beleaguered by loss and change, we keep our bearings only by clinging to remnants of stability' (ibid. p. 6). In a popular way and through commercialised lifelong learning, heritage seems to be undertaking at least some of the identity and community-building functions that in Victorian times, many writers saw as the task of formal education:

There are some things to be learned from the History of England that are of some import to the future life of a child, and are no play . . .To teach the love of our country is almost a religious duty . . . This is the feeling that has guided me in writing 'LITTLE ARTHUR'S HISTORY.

(Callcott 1878 pp. vii–viii)

By 1956, the year in which this author was born, the patriotic and nationalistic qualities engendered by children learning history had been thrown into doubt, not least by two world wars. One of the twentieth century's most popular English children's history writers could nevertheless argue that learning history made a moral contribution to 'community':

Our children are more likely to grow into citizens of the kind of race that, in our better moments, we know ourselves to be, if they have been made aware of the qualities of men and women whom successive generations have admired . . . the examples of great men and women have a fundamental value in teaching history to children.

(Unstead 1956 p. 3)

An equivalent to such 1950s moralising can be found in the curriculum 2000 statement on 'The importance of history'. Here it is assumed, in contemporary individualistic and consumerist mode, that through studying history pupils will come to '. . . see the diversity of human experience, and understand more about themselves as individuals and members of society. What they learn can influence their decisions about personal choices, attitudes and values' (DfEE 1999a p. 14). In this twenty-first century mission statement it is self-discovery, more than belonging, that a child learns through history. Individual sensibilities are emphasised but the communal belonging which so much rhetoric claims for education has, in reality, been leased to 'heritage':

Perhaps as a result of the collapse of ideas of national destiny, there is the growing importance of 'memory places' in ideas of the historical past. Landscape, and in particular those vast tracts . . . under the administration of the National Trust, is now called upon to do the memory work which in earlier times might have been performed by territorial belonging.

(Samuel 1994 p. 39)

Such a retreat into nostalgia can exacerbate contemporary alienation from feelings of care and community, exactly the qualities which the introduction of 'Citizenship' into the national curriculum is designed to promote (DfEE 1999c pp. 182–6). Perhaps more dangerously, the widespread prevalence of heritage over history can result in just the sort of simplistic 'cultural restorationist' thinking about education, identified in Chapter 3 as being so influential upon the school curriculum:

Many doubt their leaders' vision or ability to sustain a livable globe; dismayed by technology, they hark back to a simpler past whose virtues they inflate and whose vices they ignore. We show chronic affection for anything apart from the present.

(Lowenthal 1998 p. 10)

Needless to say the word 'heritage', like the term 'imagination', is nowhere to be found in the 2000 version of English national curriculum history, despite these ideas being two of the most common educational resources to which children and communities have access. As educators we must register this omission, so that our practice may compensate for it. As to exactly why this should be so, when hordes of adults and children are so patently interested in exercising their imaginations through consuming heritage, remains an alluring mystery. Clerical error, educational partiality, political conspiracy, social snobbery? Perhaps history will one day explain . . .

Englishness: Whose History and Whose Community?

History suggests that the 2000 English national curriculum, for all its twenty-first century lip gloss, is very much a nineteenth century model dressed in twentieth century clothes. Its structure, privileging ICT and aspects of English, maths and science, speaks of a reverence for traditional 'basics' inherited from the Victorian elementary tradition (Alexander 1984, 1995); reverence mixed with genuine fears that the information technology of the twenty-first century may disenfranchise and unemploy citizens who do not understand it. The 1998–9 curriculum 'consultation process' itself acknowledged at an early stage that little should change. 'Any future review must not result in disruption and upheaval to the school curriculum and schools' planning for improvement. Nor should it distract teachers from the central task of raising standards. . .' (QCA 1998 p. 9). Despite the short term, pragmatic persuasiveness of these claims, such reasoning also failed to reconcile the difficulties which the essentially unreformed structure enshrined. In terms of community these are manifold.

For instance, despite the curriculum being 'national' and emphasising throughout the importance of the 'nation state', it is fundamentally confused as to 'which nation' is consistently referred to. Over the last decade of the twentieth century Northern Ireland, Scotland and Wales continued to develop national curricula of their own. Such curricula examine these countries' individual histories. In Wales for instance, children aged 7 to 11 learn about 'Life in Early Wales and Britain, Life in Modern Wales and Britain, Life in Wales and Britain in either Stuart or Tudor Times'. They also make a local study. The curriculum for 11 to 14 year olds reflects the same perspective with only one study, that of the 20th Century world, failing to lead with a Welsh focus (ACCAC 1999).

What of the object primarily under examination in this book, the English national curriculum? It might be expected that this equivalent document would attempt a similar focus on English history as the Welsh took on Wales. This is not the case. There is no attempt in the English national curriculum for history explicitly to examine the history of 'England' as opposed to the history of 'Britain'. The term 'Britain' is mentioned four times in the requirements for KS1 and the words 'England' or 'English' not at all. At KS2 the equivalent is twenty-three mentions for 'Britain' or 'British' and one for 'England' or 'English', this being in the phrase 'aspects of the histories of England, Ireland Scotland and Wales where appropriate'. At KS3 'Britain', 'British' and the term 'United Kingdom' are mentioned eighteen times, the term 'England' or 'English' twice. The first time is in exactly the same sentence as quoted above for KS2, the second time is in the non-statutory examples for Britain 1500–1750 mentioning 'relations between England and Scotland'. In other words the story of 'England' is neither explicitly constructed nor criticised in the English national curriculum, as 'Wales' is in the Welsh. In its place is offered the misleading and even arrogant assumption that somehow 'Britain' can be English, when the government or a teacher needs it to be, but can change back to properly 'British' when more convenient.

To point this out is not to argue for an Anglo-centric curriculum ignoring local, British, European or world history; it is to expose another gap in the English national curriculum which, at the moment, only us teachers can fill. The terms 'imagination' and 'heritage' have been excluded from this 'national' curriculum. So has any searching or consistent historical examination of how an 'English' community, to which it might be supposed that most learners of an English national curriculum belong, differs from or is the same as the contentious term of 'British'. For instance, a foremost historian of 'Britishness' concluded a major work on the issue in 1992 with the argument that

> Great Britain . . . as it exists today, must be seen as one relatively new nation, and as three much older nations – with the precise relationship between these old and new alignments still changing and becoming more fiercely debated even as I write . . .What seems indisputable is that a substantial rethinking of what it means to be British can no longer be evaded.
>
> (Colley 1992 p. 374–5)

Such an evasion in schools will continue well into the new millennium, if curriculum 2000 history is not approached by teachers with a constructively critical eye. For despite much of the content of the national curriculum in history for England actually being English, it is often named as British. If Britain was a country with a future as strong as its claimed past, if the United Kingdom could live up to that adjective, would such obfuscation be needed? How can children be relaxed or positive about Englishness, when their leaders so evidently are not?

In similar fashion, the chronological structure through which most national curricular historical content for 7–14 year olds is organised militates against pursuing fundamental historical themes across broad sweeps of time. Exciting historical examinations of gender, childhood, class and ethnicity appear to be enabled by the 'knowledge, skills and understanding' requirements of national curriculum history; but are made unlikely by the fragmentation and cramming of national curriculum history into arbitrary and conventional British 'periods'. The educational structuring of history through traditional devices such as monarchy (e.g. 'Victorian Britain' or 'Britain and the wider world in Tudor times') and arbitrary periods (e.g. 'Britain 1500–1750', 'Britain 1750–1900') may suit vested interests in publishing, teaching, examining and politics, but it makes curriculum 2000 difficult to adapt to English communities' particular needs.

English history educators wanting to mediate curricula for the twenty-first century need to balance such official inertia with plenty of personal confidence, professional support and well-developed critical awareness. For they are being asked to point English children towards their future using a curriculum structure and historical content still dominated, despite cosmetic disguise, by nineteenth century visions of elementary schooling and British nationalism. Such underlying curricular structures matter not just to politicians and theorists. They also influence teachers, learners and communities and can reinforce the insensitive or arrogant behaviours which new curriculum areas such as 'citizenship' or 'PSHE' are designed to combat:

> Teachers have to be aware that life goes on among the children, often out of sight of adults . . . bullying and victimisation can occur and . . . may actually be fed by the way children distort or exploit the information they are learning through the curriculum itself. There is no guarantee that learning about the history of another culture or community will lead to tolerance . . . work on extending the history curriculum must always be part of a broader project which takes on children's and adults' attitudes and respect for each other, and is set within a framework for social justice.
>
> (Claire 1996 p. 14)

If educational history in England is to utilise its full power, teachers need to think through to whose history, and to whose community, the curriculum is ultimately responsible. Is it to a notional 'British' community which legislates for separate Scottish, Welsh and Northern Irish histories, but fudges the English equivalent under bland 'Britishness'? Or might a more diverse historical 'Englishness' be developed for English children to learn about, through a more varied curriculum? This might be harder work than the present, one-size-fits-all arrangement: but would celebrate England's multicultural past and present, alongside valuing its localities and regions. Its primary aim would be to offer children a coherent story of how Englishness fits into this varied world, at the same time as developing the intellectual skills and personal understandings with which to deconstruct it (see also Bage 2000b).

For all its blemishes, and this chapter has tried to look at the 2000 English national curriculum for history with a cold and critical eye, it is also obvious that this curriculum offers teachers and communities many opportunities to work towards enterprising and local educational ends. It is to this final issue that we now turn: the extent to which it is possible to make national curriculum history a locally educational experience.

Can History be Made Locally?

One of education's classic conundrums is that, however nationalised or standardised its systems become, the arts of teaching and the acts of learning remain resolutely local. Learning may be supported by the socialising influences of media, family, friendships, groups and interaction, but it is as individuals that people ultimately make sense of these experiences; and it is generally through the communicative power of individuals that what is learnt from one group or context is carried into the next. 'Nobody can learn it for you' us (presumably) learned adults often preach at our offspring, and students: 'you have to do it for yourself'. There is a lot of truth in that. It is possible to persuade or coerce people to *appear* as though they are learning. It is practically impossible, not to mention a contradiction in terms, to compel people to learn of their own free will. Long may it remain so. If we discovered how to force people 'willingly' to reproduce as 'learning' everything others taught them, liberty would be dead. Assuming this argument to be sound, it follows that teaching and learning at some stage must be made local: they have to be individualised and embodied, by particular people, for education to happen. 'National' knowledge, as expressed in a curriculum or regulation, is not knowledge in an educational sense: rather it is standardised information, waiting to be transformed into individual knowledge through the creative and personalising processes of teaching and learning.

This argument seems strong across many curriculum subjects but especially so in 'history'. We may be justifiably ambitious for history to foster an increased sense of a collective past; and value history's capacity to offer communities common experiences and ideas, through which they can communicate with each other about background and origins. Such commonality can nevertheless be achieved only through developing individual senses and interpretations, for it is largely as individuals that we exchange understandings with others and so participate in the commonealth of 'culture'. It is also because we are individuals that such participation is interesting. For what would be the point of exchanging meanings and ideas with others, if theirs equalled ours? The desire to discover the differences and similarities between other people and ourselves, other worlds and our own, is at the heart of human curiosity about past and present.

This view of education and culture implies 'history' starting with the local, and coming to know local history well enough to compare 'here' with 'elsewhere'. It also implies finishing with the local, being the locality of the individual who carries his or her understanding through life. It does not mean that all history taught and learnt in between is local, since the purpose of the educational enterprise is envisaged as 'exchange': exchange between past and present, individual and collective and local, regional, national and international cultures. The purpose of 'knowing the local' is to equip the learner to go beyond the locality, as well as to live within it: to offer learners local knowledge goods to barter in the national and international cultural markets visited in school or beyond. The theoretical and philosophical aspects of this argument are augmented by three practical ones.

First, the forthcoming chapters offer practical examples of how this slippery concept of the 'national' curriculum in history can be mediated by teachers to support local learning, teaching, curricula and communities. Although there is currently growing up a generation of English teachers who have known nothing but teaching within a national curriculum, they were preceded by a generation who knew nothing of it. To this older tranche of teachers, the national curriculum represented a fundamental personal and professional challenge. As the writer of this book I ought to tell you as reader, that whichever generation you believe yourself to belong to, I believe I belong to both. The forthcoming chapters also try to represent some of the 'best practice' of both, illustrating through specific advice or practical examples how teachers can critically mediate national curricula into local forms.

Second, and to its credit, the English 'national' curriculum in history has consistently asked teachers to include aspects of 'local' history. The current KS1 version envisages children studying 'changes in their own lives and the way of life of their family or others around them' alongside 'the way of life of people in the more distant past who lived in the local area', although it then goes on to demand three other categories of 'British' rather than local study (DfEE 1999b p. 16). At KS2 one of six history studies is explicitly local, alongside three British, one European and a world history study. Although there are numerous possibilities for local aspects of these studies, it is neither required nor suggested within the structure of the curriculum (ibid. pp. 18–19). At KS3 there is more scope than previously for local elements and a creative, ambitious requirement that 'Pupils should be taught . . . to identify trends, both within and across different periods, and links between local, British, European and world history' (ibid. p. 20). Various sketches supporting such an ambition follow in this book's next four chapters.

The 2000 English national curriculum in history also strengthened the require-ments, at KS2 and KS3, to embody diversity in 'the past'. For instance pupils between the ages of 7 and 11 have to be taught about 'the social, cultural, religious and ethnic diversity of the societies studied, in Britain and the wider world' (ibid. p. 17), with an identical requirement at KS3. Both key stages emphasise the importance of women and children in history, as well as men. Between the ages of 11 and 14 students also have to study history from a 'variety of perspectives including political, religious, social, cultural, aesthetic, economic, technological and scientific' (ibid. p. 21). Although all these requirements have to be viewed through the mandatory prism of British and largely conventional history studies, they allow creative curricular scope for local interpretations and emphases.

Third, it is possible to encounter the past largely through the local *and* to improve learners' written and spoken language proficiency *and* to motivate students who may be personally disaffected and culturally or socially alienated from the curriculum. From America comes one example of how these highly desirable ends can be achieved. The 'Foxfire' project started life in 1966, as a student and teacher-published magazine publishing local stories and oral histories, from the Appalachian mountains. It is still working and has spread far beyond its original high school into a national, high-profile educational and publishing project. Here, a female student talks of how local history learned the Foxfire way changed her view of herself and others:

> Foxfire showed that those old people weren't just dumb old hillbillies . . . It
> made me feel proud to be a part of that, a part of a culture that they came out

of. I never really ever knew what my heritage was until I got into Foxfire. It seems like I had a lot more in common with these older people than I had thought. It was like you've got a thumb here but you've never paid any attention to it. It was like something that's been there but I never realised it was part of me.

(Wigginton 1998 p. 210, first published 1988)

Meanwhile, the originator of the project was expressing grave doubts about Foxfire replicas that had sprung up around the USA. It seemed to him that many of these school and university spin-offs had adopted the outer form of the original, but misunderstood or ignored its inner logic. At Foxfire's heart lay:

. . . our attempt to answer the universal student question, 'Why are you making us sit here and *do* this?' In response, we try to bring the academic agenda to life as students use the items on that agenda in the solution of real problems, or the creation of real products that our community values and applauds.

(Wigginton 1989 p. 26)

A summary of the '10 common ingredients' of this philosophy is included in Chapter 8, together with examples of how they may be mediated for application within the English national curriculum in history. This is not to suggest that teaching in 'Foxfire' or related ways can ever be easy. As two teacher–educators commented after revolutionising their initial teacher education course through Foxfire principles 'Using the Foxfire approach takes a maturity and desire for change that challenges the most experienced teacher' (Dittmer and Fischetti 1995 p. 172). As they also commented, over half of the United States existing teacher workforce seemed so challenged by life in conventional classrooms that they left teaching anyway after 6 years, proportions currently similar to those in England. It may be a greater and far less satisfying challenge to sustain these educational systems, squandering teachers as they do, than radically to change them in ways that Foxfire principles suggest.

Initiatives using local and oral history within the English national curriculum are common and I have touched on some elsewhere (see Bage 1999a). In the space available here I would like briefly to mention two other ways of thinking which teachers can use to localise and enliven the national history curriculum. The first is epitomised by the writings of Sylvia Collicott (Collicott 1986, 1990, 1992, 1993). Working before and after the introduction of the national curriculum, she showed how conventional historical studies could be transformed into more balanced and rigorous educational experiences by making local, national and world links. The focus could be a place (e.g. Haringey, Collicott 1986), resulting in an incredibly rich collection of challenging historical material. Or, it could be a national curriculum-required KS2 study such as 'Britain since 1930' which currently requires primary teachers to lead 'a study of the impact of the Second World War or social and technological changes that have taken place since 1930 . . .' (DfEE 1999a p. 18). The national curriculum demands that 'pupils should be taught about . . . social, cultural, religious and ethnic diversity' (ibid. p. 17). Collicott's work shows how this can be done, without pretending that it is easy. Using an intriguing combination of national and personal threads to construct a timeline of the 1940s and 1950s, she demonstrated how the experience of women and children and the 'colonial contribution' (Collicott 1992 p. 259) can be given due weight, resulting in history that is more personal and therefore engaging for students, as well as more racially, culturally and socially balanced. Changing the nature of reference books may help achieve this but is only half the job, the rest being to develop pedagogy and resources so as to bring 'a diversity of content and evidence to children' (ibid. p. 252). Teachers have to take the lead in this:

> Teachers can only teach new information which they themselves have learned. Similarly children can only learn new ideas if their teachers have learned them too. Once the timeline of facts about the war has been established in the classroom, perhaps by asking children to select some of the facts they found of interest in their reference books, it is possible to fit other facts in.
>
> (ibid. p. 259)

Collicott's ideas epitomise the culturally transactional nature of history teaching, as being a process in which teachers and children use 'national' referential frameworks such as books, television and the national curriculum, within which to construct understandings local to an age group and community.

The second, locally led way of thinking about the curriculum to sketch here is the TASTE project, which the author directs: TASTE being an acronym for teaching-as-story-telling. The TASTE project has two central aims. The first is to promote teaching and learning through storytelling. The second is to develop local stories which can be told or read, and which reach out to the wider world. Professional storytellers have been working with children, teachers, parents and community institutions to develop this work, most consistently in the London Borough of Greenwich and in the Norfolk town of King's Lynn. Some of this work has been written about elsewhere (e.g. Bage 1999a, Bage 2000a, 2000b, Collins 1999, Collins 2000), aspects of it can be seen in the following chapters, and TASTE's work continues.

TASTE has coined the term 'storyseeds' to describe the origins of the local-global stories it develops. In other words, people in the project search for something interesting in a locality such as a place, name, anecdote or person. Having found it they then use research to amass information around that storyseed; analysis to evaluate that information; and imagination to weave the information into a local-global story, that may just be 'real'. In the making, telling and retelling of such stories, the aim is for children to learn not only about their locality and how its diversity fits with the wider world; but to understand something of how 'culture' and 'curriculum' come to be constructed through disciplines such as history, science and literature. In Greenwich, the following ten stories in particular have been the focus of research, teaching and learning:

The Millennium Ten: Local–Global Stories from Greenwich

Century	Storyseed	Title (and Main Historical Sources)
11th	The name of St Alfege's School	Thrum the Viking (the Anglo-Saxon chronicle, Norse myths)
12th	Lesnes Abbey ruins	The legend of Roesia's heart (guide books, ruins, local legends and oral history)
16th	An early Tudor picture of a Black musician riding a horse	The king's trumpeter (1511 Westminster Tournament Roll)
17th	Phineas Pett Road in Eltham – a street name local to a project school	The story of Phineas Pett (Pepys diaries, reference books)
18th	'Longitude' – the best selling book by Dava Sobel	Harrison's Clocks (Sobel's book, collections at Greenwich Royal Observatory)
18th	Ignatius Sancho education pack	The 7 ages of Sancho (published materials within this pack such as pictures, documents)
19th	Edith Nesbit – a class's name from Briset School	Pandora's Box (a photograph of Edith Nesbit with her granddaughter)
19th	Women's history	Eliza Adelaide Knight (biography by her daughter)
20th	Thistlebrook travellers' site in Greenwich	The story of Bubbles Brazil (interview and oral history)
20th	Stephen Lawrence's murder in Eltham	Some of Stephen's Stories (interview with Stephen's mother Doreen)

We shall now therefore return to 'Greenwich', as one of the underlying metaphors of this book. Greenwich, you may recall in the introduction, occupies many cultural locations. It is archetypal England, stuffed with traditional museums, acres of heritage and a millennium dome. It is the anchor of longitude, linking the world in an apparently common time which triggered the new Christian millennium. Greenwich abounds with local-global stories, the ten above being a fraction of its themes; but Greenwich wears a grim face, too. This face shows what happens when the cultural and historical identities offered to some young people are so weak they fail to function, or so unattractive they are rejected. The void is filled by storyseeds of a malignant kind, as chillingly revealed through evidence presented in the Macpherson Report (1999 p. 40).

Many readers will recall that five white adolescents were the main suspects in the racist murder of a black teenager, Stephen Lawrence, in Eltham High Street in 1993. At the time of the murder they were 16 and 17 years old. Some of the group's conversations were taped whilst they were under surveillance in late 1994. This evidence, laced with violent bigotry and paraded some eighteen months after the Lawrence murder, shows racism as a culture: a way for these young men to think about themselves and others, not an isolated or one off 'incident'. Disturbingly, research in the same area and period suggested that it was peer group more than family expectations which maintained such a culture in Greenwich:

Young people moving into these neighbourhoods from more ethnically varied parts of the borough attested to the gradual but distinctive influence that the extreme and widespread racism of the local youth had on them. The racism of adolescents was a world of its own, policed from within. . .

(Hewitt 1996 p. 27)

Why include such examples here, in a book on history and the national curriculum? Why introduce it in this section, on history and community?

Not because history, curricula, teachers or even education can alone 'solve' these problems: but because without sensitive, intelligent and localised attempts to build historical identity from the inside, from within schools and families and learners, this author sees little chance of building the proud, multicultural and local English historical identity which he passionately believes can counteract racism. As was argued a few pages back, students can encounter national history largely through the local *and* improve their written and spoken language *and* pursue genuine enquiries *and* be motivated to do so, even if they start off feeling personally, culturally or socially alienated from school. What students cannot do is to achieve such things simply through having national curriculum history 'applied' to them: a curriculum which, at least in content terms, fabricates a supposedly 'national' but suspiciously mythic 'British' history.

Might Greenwich be a metaphor for a new kind of educational history? Not in the hope of standardising everything along the same meridian lines, but of celebrating the distinctive diversities of English society through its schools and communities. After the arguments made in the first four chapters of this book, such a refutation of standardisation should come as no great surprise. What follows in the next few chapters are examples of how, in practical terms, the incomplete and occasionally dangerous idea of a 'national' history curriculum can be mediated and improved by teachers' practices.

Section 2
Introspect

5　Learning History in Practice

A. Why Learn History?

To be effective in history teaching we need to articulate to our own and our school's satisfaction what children gain from learning history. The national curriculum helps with such thinking but does not do it for us. Nor is there a single way of structuring the history curriculum: schools can individualise it.

This policy statement is designed as a model which schools can adapt to create their own policy document (Figure 5.1). It has been developed through practice in different LEAs and with a range of schools. It helps us consider this book's following underlying questions:

- *Does history teaching challenge or implement a school's stated aims for learning history?*
- *How are history curricula inter-disciplinary or subject-specific?*
- *Are history curricula locally or nationally defined?*
- *Do history curricula reveal or obscure the grounds for history's claims to value?*

Figure 5.1　A policy statement for history

1　The nature of history

We use the word history in two ways. Its simple meaning is an all-embracing term for 'the past' covering everything before now. As a more complex term 'history' also describes how we find out about, imagine and communicate our picture of this past, by studying, observing, questioning etc. History in school is largely about helping children move from the simple to the more complex definition. As they do so history can become an exciting and lifelong window on the world.

History invites children to think about past human existence using a wide range of skills and faculties. Since history is used to make sense of time and to order human actions, it draws on ideas that children encounter through the many forms and uses of story. Indeed, history can be explained to children as 'using questions and evidence to take apart and put together again real stories about the past'.

Children need to know why we learn about this thing called history, if they are going to become enthusiastic about doing so. Our lessons and schemes of work should always open this to discussion.

2　The aims of history

As children grow older they develop a clearer idea of the outline of the past: but on

---

its own this is not history. Learning history rests upon acquiring and being able to analyse their knowledge about historical content, ideas and evidence. In this light the 'breadth of study' requirements in national curriculum history are stepping stones rather than ends in themselves. The 'knowledge, skills and understanding' aspects of the national curriculum programmes of study (below) and the personal qualities, attitudes and values developed through history (section 3) are of equal importance. These fuel children to learn through and move beyond any particular piece of historical content.

The 'knowledge, skills and understanding' aspects of national curriculum history (KSU) clarify the thinking skills and abilities that learning history helps children to develop. In this document they have been extended and renamed, but are referred to in their national curricular form by the numbering in the DfEE (1999a) document:

KSU1 Chronological understanding
KSU2 Knowledge and understanding of events, people and changes in the past
KSU3 Historical interpretation
KSU4 Historical enquiry
KSU5 Organisation and communication

History promotes:
(a) *Problem-solving and questioning* skills, both to decide what the problem is ('what can we find out about our school 100 years ago?') and to work out questions within a problem ('why did these children arrive from London in 1940?'). (KSU4)
(b) *Analytical* abilities, by asking children to examine evidence ('how can you tell what has happened to this old house over the years?'). (KSU4)
(c) *Explaining and interpreting* most easily in storied or question and answer forms ('tell me the story of how railways changed people's lives' or more simply 'what happened during the Fire of London?'). (KSU2)
(d) *Conceptual* acquisition and thinking especially about time, chronology, change, continuity, cause, consequence, comparison, interpretations and evidence ('how do modern Olympic games compare to the ancient Greeks?') (KSU1, 2)
(e) *Communicative* abilities as children use spoken, written and visual languages to examine and express views of history. History in schools involves a variety of media ('make a display, tell a story, give a talk, write an article about') which shape as well as communicate historical ideas. (KSU4, 5)
(f) *Knowledge* acquisition and confidence. Historical knowledge is virtually limitless. Such abundance requires sensitive handling by teachers but all children of whatever previous attainment can learn and apply 'study skills' in history ('use the encyclopedia or CD ROM to discover as much as you can about the ancient Mayans'). ('breadth of study' requirements, KSU2 especially)
(g) *Judgement-making* because by nature, history is an incomplete form of knowledge. History ends as well as begins with some unanswered questions ('why do you think people did cave paintings?'). (KSU2, 3, 4)
(h) *Inter-disciplinary* abilities. Science, art, language, music, DT, geography, ICT and RE are well represented in the human past. History can enhance or be the focus for inter-disciplinary school projects ('this term we are finding out about castles and we shall be dancing, painting, model-making, cooking and making music as we go. . .'). (KSU2, 4, 5 especially)

3 Spiritual, moral, social and cultural development
The curriculum as a whole, and history in particular, supports the development of

individual children's personal qualities, attitudes and values. It fosters their sense of community involvement and identity, leading to more confident and engaged senses of citizenship. By their learning of history we hope to stimulate children's:

(a) *Curiosity* about past and different cultures.
(b) *Sense of identities* from personal through to national.
(c) *Tolerance* of the many values, cultures and peoples from past and present.
(d) *Respect* for past and present achievements and sacrifices.
(e) *Imagination* fuelled and tempered by evidence.
(f) *Critical abilities* to question claims made in texts and other media.
(g) *Understanding and interpretations* of the present.
(h) *Ethical awareness* through discussing historical 'rights and wrongs.'
(i) *Empowerment* through historical slants on citizenship, multicultural awareness, sustainable development or aspects of personal, social and health education.
(j) *A sense of plurality* because history is full of rich human diversities.
(k) *Senses of common identity* in tension with the above.
(l) *A capacity for puzzlement* or living with ambiguity.
(m) *A desire to make meaning*, which is a fundamental of motivated, effective learning.

4   Time allocation for history

History is taught for approximately 36 hours per year at KS1 and 45 hours per year at KS2 and 60 hours per year at KS3.

5   Contribution to the whole curriculum for all children

History can be made accessible and challenging for all children if teachers are confident in their own knowledge, deploy a variety of teaching styles and offer access to a range of resources.

Within the bounds of the National Curriculum we teach history in depth so that all children can construct explanations from interesting and sometimes differentiated resources and evidence. In-depth historical investigations handling diverse information and evidence gives children the maximum opportunity to develop the six key skills of: communication, application of number, information technology, working with others, improving their own learning and performance and problem solving. They also involve children in developing 'thinking skills' closely allied to the historical process: information-processing, reasoning, enquiry, creative thinking and evaluation.

As well as supporting these broad skills leaning history improves:

- the development of oracy and literacy;
- the purposeful use of ICT;
- links with parents and the community through open evenings, local studies, visits and visitors.

6   Assessment, recording and reporting

Individual progress in history will be assessed, marked, recorded and reported to parents in accordance with school policy. The different aspects of historical 'knowledge, skills and understanding' described in the national curriculum form the basis for formative assessments and are the foundation for the summative assessments made via national curriculum history level descriptions.

Question or command words such as *'who, how, what, where, why, when, in what order, which, if, whether, did, can, try, find, search, could, might, research, enquire, should, choose, because, since, compare, think, remember, tell, explain, show, list, order, imagine, what if, what else'* will be used as the basis for planning teaching and assessing learning in history. Assessment will be through spoken as well as written means.

7 Monitoring and review

The curriculum leader for history, in consultation with senior staff, will make arrangements for monitoring the implementation of this policy and the schemes of work, and ensure that dates are published for the review of documentation and the next phase of development.

B. Learning Varieties

History is an activity that distinguishes humanity, because other creatures have little conscious sense of their past: but what sort of human identities and skills are involved in history learning and teaching?

There are surprisingly diverse roles through which history learners can immerse themselves in the discipline. Nichol and Dean (1997 p. 50) enumerate some and this study of varieties of learning extends their work by drawing upon the author's own practice and research. Not all roles are appropriate for everybody and it would be foolish to offer learners too many at one time. Equally, the unitary appearance of the document describing English national curriculum history does not reflect the diversity of how that curriculum can be learnt about, in practice.

The second part of the document blends important ideas from research about learning with observations from the practice of history teaching. Its ideas were first used in a 9–13 middle school in 1994 and have since been refined. The third section offers practical classroom suggestions for improving 'differentiation' in history learning.

The document may be especially useful for considering these underlying questions:

- *Does history learning develop multiple or singular intelligences?*
- *Does it start from the curriculum's requirements or different children's needs?*
- *Whether history teaching standardises or differentiates pedagogy and materials?*

Different roles for history learners

Learning about history can be achieved using many different roles. These can be chosen to reflect the preferences of children and teachers and the nature of the historical material being learnt about. There are four basic practical principles through which to interpret such roles (see Figure 5.2). These are that teachers should foster history learning by:

- Assembling a range of history evidence (sources) and other materials (resources) to support children's investigations;

- Stimulating children to ask searching questions, amass information, analyse evidence and where possible collect their own;
- Negotiating the activity's timescale and outcome, from short discussion through to lengthy structured role-play;
- Helping children to structure historical understandings and interpretations as presentations in forms appropriate to the investigation.

Figure 5.2   Different roles for history learners

Types of history	Learner in role as . . .
Mysteries in histories	Investigator: what questions are we trying to answer? Photographer/artist: what needs illustrating and how should it be done? Search team: what are we looking for and how should it be recorded? Scene of crime officer: how should the investigation be managed and recorded? Press officer: what should be communicated to tell other people what is happening? Forensic scientist: how do we analyse the evidence gathered? Interviewing officer: who should we question, what should we ask and how should it be recorded? Lawyers: how would we defend or prosecute those involved in this case?
History in families	Family historian: which family are we finding out about and who shall we ask? Archivist: where shall we look for clues and how will we store the evidence collected? Local historian: how can we use a church, chapel or other holy place to find out about families? Writers and illustrators: how shall we present our family histories through photographs and writing?
History in our school or community	Surveyors: what order were the different parts of our school or town built in? Interviewers: who used to attend our school or live in our village? Investigators: what do documentary sources tell us about our school or community? Authors: how can we present our history once it is compiled and who will read it?
History in biography	The publisher: what book or TV programme would sell for this period of history? The author: what do I need to find out and write up? The illustrator: what pictures can I find for this biography and how should it be presented on the cover? The researcher: where can I find enough information from which to make a good story? The editor: how can this history be sold and presented?

Types of history	Learner in role as . . .
Archaeology	The field archaeologist: how are things found, dug up and recorded? The conservator: how are fragments or objects conserved? The curator: where can we store an object and what might an object do in a display? The illustrator: what can we tell from looking at this object and how can we reconstruct it?
The historical story teller	Will this story be real or made up? How can the story be made as convincing as possible? Which characters or happenings in this story need historical research? What forms shall this story be told in? (e.g. play, poem, story, description, cartoon, mural, photographs, film) How can we plan to tell it through storyboarding? How can we tell it and sell it? What do we think of our audience's reactions?
History in the newspaper	The editor: what is the important story for this time and audience? Our journalists: what is the angle or interest in this story? The photographer: who or what should be photographed and how will I make it interesting? The sub-editors: what should this story's headline be and how does it fit with the rest of the paper? The commercial manager: what adverts can I sell in this newspaper?
History at the auction house or antique shop	The expert: what is this object and how can I find out its history? The publications department: what will our catalogue tell people about objects to entice them to attend an auction? The auctioneer: what can I say about this object to encourage people to bid? The customers: what are we looking for when we buy old objects and how do we decide what they are worth?
History in the museum	The trustees: what is this museum trying to collect and why? The curators: what is important in my collection and which parts should I put on show? The illustrators: how can these objects be presented attractively and what should texts about them say? The guides: if people ask me about an object what do I tell them and how can I explain things simply? The commercial manager: how can we sell things to people who are visiting our museum or website?
History at the college	The lecturers: how can we make our teaching more interesting? The senior management team: which history courses shall we provide to attract new learners to evening classes? The publicity department: what should advertising posters and brochures say about these history courses?

Types of history	Learner in role as . . .
	The students: what shall we tell our teachers to help them make history more interesting?
History and local government	The councillors: how can we use history to raise the profile of our town and attract in new businesses?
	The community workers: what can we find in our local history to help fight racism?
	The youth workers: are there any stories from history to show local young people's achievements in the past?
	The artists: what community art projects would help people feel more involved with the history of this place?
	The Tourist Board: what is attractive about this locality to encourage tourists from home and abroad?
History and broadcasting	The schedulers and commissioners: what history programmes should we commission for next year, and for what kinds of audience?
	The directors: what guidance should be given to researchers, script writers and actors about the history programme we are making?
	The actors: what can we learn from rehearsing and researching about how our characters would have behaved in the past?
	The researchers: what historical information would make this programme accurate but also entertaining?
	The script writers: what historical information should be included or omitted and how should this story be told?

Adapting learning theory for history

> . . . knowledge is not a commodity existing in some pure and abstract realm independently of particular knowers, but a state of understanding achieved through the constructive mental activity of individual learners . . . knowledge does not enter the mind of the learner in the form transmitted; rather, learners progressively construct their own knowledge. . . never a straightforward copy, but a new, personal reconstruction.
>
> Gordon Wells in *Thinking Voices* (ed. K. Norman 1992 p. 286)

We can make two deductions from what Wells claims:

1 Learners *individualise* knowledge by reconstructing it.
2 Learning *is individual* because people have different characteristics.

Learning styles

These reconstructions and characteristics can be described in the four ways that Kolb (1976) identified as distinctive 'learning styles'. Such styles relate to approaches, not character-types, although as individuals we may favour one approach. Part of becoming educated is acquiring versatility and being able to think in these different ways:

- Converging: practical thinking which tends to focus on a single issue and look for a solution. Convergent thinkers like to experiment in active and methodical ways, working their way through questions and solutions;
- Diverging: thinking which aims to understand more than solve a problem, looking at it in broad context and finding original approaches.
- Assimilating: thinking which values abstract concepts and models highly, often developing models to assimilate all available data into a new theory.
- Accommodating: pragmatic thinking searching for effective strategies and tactics, emphasising versatility, impact and relevance.

How does this help teachers to plan learning?

3   We need to design teaching and learning which allows children to individualise their understanding in different ways. Using Kolb's theory this can lead to planning for history learning in terms of concrete experience, reflective observation, abstract conceptualisation and active experimentation. If we plan a curriculum touching upon all of these, there is a good chance it will be successful for more children.

4   There are different 'scales' in which this balance can assist curriculum design:

- as an individual teacher (e.g. do I employ a rich mix in lessons and units?)
- as a year group of teachers (e.g. do we offer variety over a year?)
- in a subject (e.g. does history in this school draw upon different learning styles and offer different sorts of challenge?)
- in a Key Stage (e.g. is our 'KS3 history curriculum' too abstract and reflective?)
- as a whole school (e.g. how do we monitor whether we stretch and support all learners?)

5   The scale over which we have most everyday control is the first. As an individual teacher, do I employ a rich mix? Some variables are:

- how a lesson connects to the last one and leads to the next one, and whether this is communicated clearly to children;
- resources (type, range, quantity, quality, accessibility etc.);
- learner grouping (individual, paired, small group, large group, whole class by subject, social skills or linguistic attainment);
- teacher expectations of children clearly communicated (expressed in tasks planned and set, language, attitudes, arrangement of classroom, displays, questions asked etc.);
- teacher language (spoken, written, pitch, pace, code, interest, balance of analysis and anecdote etc.);
- types of task set: 'work' in and across subjects which demands learning through different styles such as concrete experience, reflective observation, abstract conceptualisation and active experimentation;

- outcomes expected from tasks set (e.g. spoken, written, read, observed, quantified, made, designed, illustrated, mimed, danced, performed, remembered, etc.);
- teacher feedback (verbal, written, expressed, formative, summative, collaborative, positive, critical, punitive, etc.);
- timescales set and stuck to (2 minutes to half a term to a whole school career).

What other strategies can I use to help history appeal to different learners?

Formative assessment can be planned into lessons and units to help break down broad requirements into tasks that are clearer or more easily attainable for learners and teachers. The following techniques can assist this:

- use '*all* of the class – *most* of the class – *some* of the class' as a device to plan for differentiated coverage at the start of a study, or to help evaluate it at the end.
- use '*with a lot of help – a little help – independently*' as a key to help children assess for themselves which elements of 'knowledge, skills and understanding' they feel confident about.
- use the prompts '*I can do . . . I know . . . I want to enquire about . . . I do not understand*' as starting points for children's oral or written self-assessments in history.

Common tasks can be set for a whole group, anticipating that they will show different levels of understanding by outcome eg 'draw pictures to compare an office today with one of 150 years ago'. This can be effective if the task is clear, attainable and open ended enough for individuals to interpret it at different levels. In the wording of the task use key conceptual, skills-based or content words from the history curriculum to make the history objectives clear to everybody.

Different tasks can be set for groups or individuals e.g.:

- core common task, extension activities just for some;
- stepped tasks in a series of increasingly hard historical questions;
- students asked to devise their own historical questions or tasks;
- students themselves choose what to answer from a list of varying historical questions.

Varied resources and evidence can be deployed e.g.:

- different language levels for different groups of pupils, whether in information books or your own evidence and information sheets;
- conceptually harder historical evidence given to some students;
- more or less varied sources of historical evidence to students;

- less or more conflicting historical evidence according to prior attainment and confidence;
- different sources of secondary historical information to students eg.some go to library, use computer, have textbooks, watch TV, etc.

Timing can individualise learning. Ask groups to undertake related or similar tasks, to enable the teacher to talk to the whole class at key points: but allocate different amounts of time and numbers of tasks.

Sensitive talk helps learners, which most teachers do intuitively with individuals or groups. We vary the pace, simplicity, tone and content of our talk to adjust to the level of understanding of our listeners. This is particularly important in history for two reasons:

- some of the language involves arcane concepts such as time, religion, causation, which need simple presentation for effect;
- others words are apparently simple, such as 'queen', 'castle', 'law', but their meanings change over time and will not be the same as a modern child might understand.

Group organisation can vary from year and class groups, to discussion groups of 4/5, to trios, pairs and individuals. Over a term students should experience all of these in history with appropriate tasks to match. Grouping can be decided on many criteria: previous spoken or written historical attainments, behaviour in groups, gender, pupil choice, random choice. It is particularly important in history to recognise and celebrate curiosity, enquiry and historical knowledge, none of which are necessarily correlative with the above. History can stimulate unexpected responses from unpromising students, especially when an easily accessible prompt is used such as an object, picture, talk or story.

Varying support can be offered such as using support staff, volunteer classroom helpers, visitors or team teaching to target different groups at various times.

Teaching styles should be varied over a key stage or school, so that students have the opportunity to respond at some time in ways that are accessible and positive for them (eg.use historical classroom drama, discussion, music, worksheets, artefacts, reference books for some, but not all of the time).

Listening to students and being aware of their histories is vital for fine teaching. Students struggle for many reasons: affective, cognitive, physical, cultural, economic . . . etc! Whilst it is unrealistic to expect over-stretched teachers to carry hundreds of individual case-records around in our heads, all courses should contain some negotiated elements to allow for some individualisation of preferred learning styles, paces, etc.

C. On Knowing (and Not Knowing) in History

Alexander, Schallert and Hare (1991) reviewed over 300 books and articles describing international research on learning and literacy: they wanted to find out what researchers meant by 'knowledge'. Having discovered a diversity of terms and knowledges, plural, they analysed and named them. Their analysis helps us think about learning history: and to reconsider what we mean by knowing, and not knowing, history.

They argue that knowledge is individualistic, dynamic and interactive, being in any single learner a mixture of some different types described below. I have offered examples for history within their typology of knowledges (see Figure 5.3) and then considered some important barriers that studying and teaching history can throw up for learners. This paper supports teachers considering history, special educational needs and literacy. It is especially useful in considering this book's following underlying questions:

- *Should history teaching adhere to predicted plans and objectives or respond to children's needs?*
- *Do history curricula advance multimedia or only written literacy skills?*
- *Are communities comprehensive or selective in their aspirations for history?*
- *Does history learning develop multiple or singular intelligences?*

Figure 5.3   Type of formal knowledge

Conceptual knowledge – Knowing about ideas, about how and when to use them (e.g. historical change, causation, interpretation).

Content knowledge – Knowing about an aspect of the physical, social or mental world. Encompasses discipline (e.g. history), domain (e.g. school history) and declarative (knowing what – factual information) knowledge.

Discourse knowledge – Knowing about the language to use when discussing particular content or conceptual knowledge (e.g. understanding and using historical terms, making an historical argument, telling an historical story). Encompasses word, syntactic, text-structure and rhetorical knowledge.

Metacognitive knowledge – Knowing about knowing: knowledge of tasks, self, plans and goals, procedures and strategies for knowing (e.g. knowing about being educated in history: how to use a book, discuss a document, analyse a picture, survive a lesson, pass an exam, undertake enquiry).

Prior knowledge – Knowing what one knows now: the sum of personal knowledge that informs approaches to new knowledge (i.e. what makes us individual, Hexter's 'second record', the life history of respondents and interviewers in oral history, the values informing historians' interpretations). Often referred to as our 'experience'.

Knowledge sites and sorts
Construction – Where prior, conceptual and metacognitive knowledge meet to enhance an individual's understanding, interpretation or representation. Sometimes referred to as instantiation (e.g. when a question, comment or experience sparks off a new personal understanding of the past).

> *Sociocultural knowledge* – A filter through which all other knowledge passes, based on tacit understandings between members of groups (e.g. nations, gangs, professional groups such as historians or teachers, schools and classes).
>
> *Explicit knowledge* – Knowledge that is brought to consciousness, open to planned deployment and made public and accountable (e.g. the sort of knowledge claimed in a formal presentation or written answer describing an aspect of someone's historical knowledge).
>
> *Tacit knowledge* – Knowledge that is available for use but which is not conscious. This often informs judgements on an everyday basis (e.g. personal or professional intuition about history, affective judgements about the past, subconscious or concealed reasons stemming from life history for particular interests or views in an individual).

Why do some students not know their history? (even when teachers try hard)

There are some sources of educational failure which individually, teachers can do little to control such as physical wellbeing, social conditions or economic hardship: others we *do* have more control over. Alexander, Schallert and Hare's 'foundations and types of knowledge' provide a framework to talk about these, as does analysing our own experience of teaching. Problems may include:

1   History's *conceptual knowledge* (the national curriculum's 'knowledge, skills and understanding') appears to students only as abstract ideas rather than as powerful forces shaping the lives around them. Fostering the desire to know, stemming from feelings and affection, is as important as acquiring the skills to know.

2   History's *content knowledge* (touched on throughout the national curriculum) does not motivate students to want to construct their own understandings with it. This is especially the case where conceptual knowledge has been taught poorly. Typically such poor teaching leaves lower-attaining students unclear about the processes they are trying to follow and higher-attaining students bored by them.

3   History's *discourse knowledge* has not been translated, taught or eased by us as teachers. Consequently, the linguistic demands of history as a school subject seem impossibly high, especially when teacher language does not tempt a student into, or open up the subject. Some typical difficulties are that:

   • history's specialist register becomes incomprehensible without specialist knowledge to embody it (e.g. sovereignty, guild, colonisation);
   • history's specialist register can be ambiguous where it is simpler (e.g. church, party, social, crown);
   • original materials in historical materials are frequently inaccessible (not being written for students or the twenty-first century);
   • word meanings change over time (e.g. factory, crusade, want);
   • history uses colligations as though they were actual and concrete (e.g. feudalism, Christianity, Black Death, trade, monarchy);

- textbooks are linguistically compressed (e.g. they typically cover wide periods or themes in as few a pages as possible, they mimic reference books rather than enquiry manuals);
- history writers complicate and depersonalise explanations in pursuit of balance and objectivity (e.g. two points of view are considered, or a 'third person' stance adopted without giving readers access to the original materials from which a balance was drawn).

4   Many schools do not teach *metacognitive knowledge* well. They often:

- assume a clear idea or prior knowledge of what history is and for, when such an understanding does not exist or has altered;
- assume that students know how to do things independently when they cannot e.g. take notes, read textbooks, discuss ideas, work in groups, understand terminology, listen to explanations, construct interpretations, make judgements, etc;
- attempt to teach skills in the point above disembodied from an actual and meaningful investigation – ensuring that the learning is both unrealistic and temporary.

5   Because of a host of reasons, schools often ignore pupils' *prior knowledge*:

- lack of internal or external liaison meaning that learning achievements in history are lost or ignored;
- ignoring or mis-hearing pupils when they do respond (e.g. with anecdotes, discussion of television or computer games that appear linked, affective judgements);
- assuming too much understanding of history (e.g. this group has not asked any questions so they must understand) or too little potential (e.g. this group are lower-attainers in language so they will be in history).

6   Learning does not appropriately draw together the elements needed for *knowledge construction*. Perhaps teachers use an insufficient diversity of teaching ideas, methods, resources and approaches so that the content of lessons appears distant, dull or both. Or there is such a plethora of approaches that it is hard for a student to see how all of their different experiences can be constructed together into a conceptual whole.

7   History appears to have different *socio-cultural knowledge* and therefore alien values and filters to those commonly within some students' experience. People from the past as presented in national curricula or textbooks can easily appear 'posh, old and boring' or 'dead/white/ European/male' or 'all kings and queens'. Sex, death and toilets are *displaced* by social and cultural history, rather than *being* them: the 'national' curriculum looks as though it belongs to somebody else's nation.

8   History appears to demand only *explicit knowledge* of the formal and rational kind, when life teaches students as well as adults that 'real' social worlds such as club, shop or factory do not value such knowledge as highly. Expressing explicit knowledge about history also relies upon developing imaginative and linguistic skills which may be absent in some learners.

9   Students' *tacit knowledge* (e.g. about friendships, families, feelings, formed
     from television or play) is often ignored or devalued by school history. This is
     especially true when learning history is presented as accumulating a
     depersonalised body of abstract knowledge rather than an exploration of the
     past through individuals' eyes and experiences. Most learners know about
     people before they know about history. History is about people who happen
     to be in the past. Learning history should feel like it is learning about people
     so that students have an inbuilt advantage.

*Readers may recognise these ways of knowing and not knowing history
from their own experiences, either as learners or teachers.
What others could be added?*

D. Questioning History?

Educational history starts with questions, not content. Historical content is
prescribed in the English National Curriculum, as compulsory periods or
episodes listed under 'Breadth of Study'. On their own these sketches are 'the
past', not 'history'. Such content needs opening through questioning, generally
with ideas in the sister section describing historical 'knowledge, skills and
understanding'. Using questions and concepts, children's classroom activities
about the past can be turned into historical understanding. When these are
considered alongside the overall aims and purposes of the national curriculum
(DfEE 1999b pp. 10–13) a powerful blend of questions, content and values can
be achieved.

Teacher-language is pivotal in this process. By modelling the thinking
processes of history out loud in our talk, or on the page in our writing, teachers
can reveal something of what history is. By simplifying or changing words, we can
make these ideas more accessible. This section therefore offers models for the
types of questions teachers can and should be asking in history. Many are open-
ended and cannot be answered with a mere 'yes' or 'no'? They have been under
development for the past five years and used with various groups of history
teachers, although the responsibility for errors and repetition rests solely with
the author.

Of course if children have been taught well already, many will arrive with
questions of their own. These are often more educationally valuable than a
teacher's questions, even though they may not be as purely 'historical'.

The examples here are drawn from the KS1 and KS2 programmes of study,
although the types of question match many KS3 needs. They are particularly
relevant to the following underlying questions in this book:

* Whether history learning aims for knowledge through questioning or
  memorisation?
* Is pursued for intrinsic or extrinsic needs?
* How history teaching adheres to predictive plans and objectives or responds
  to children's needs?

Questions to build historical knowledge, skills and understanding

1   Chronological understanding

How can we tell which of these objects might have been used a long time ago?

Can we put these pictures or objects in order and explain our choice, with the oldest first and the most recent last? (e.g. *relating to transport, buildings, armour, costume*).

Which of these things might your grandparents have used? (*Provide a list or assortment of materials, e.g. household goods.*) Explain how you chose.

Read the story. What changes happened to the hero or heroine during the time of the story?

What does this (*artefact/book/picture, etc.*) tell us about (*cooking, transport, entertainment, etc.*) when your grandparents were young?

How could we find out about how life has changed in (*schools, villages, factories, etc.*) over the last (*50, 1000, 100 years*)?

From historical pictures of place:

How can we tell at what time in history this picture might have been taken?

How can we work out what age most of the things shown in this picture come from?

What are the newest/oldest things we can see here?

What is shown *now* that might not have been around *then*?

What might have been there *then* that has disappeared *now*?

Dates and vocabulary

What useful words do we know to help find out about history?

How many words describing time can we think of?

How many words describing what time does to things can we think of?

What does this (*costume, toy, piece of furniture, etc.*) tell us about how long ago it might have been made?

Can we turn these words (*from a list appropriate for KS1 or KS2*) into questions about things from the past? (*a picture, artefact, etc.*)

Choose a word or phrase from this list to say when you think this object was made (*e.g. one thousand years ago, last year, about fifty years ago OR when my mum was young/when my grandad was young/before my grandad was born*).

2   *Knowledge and understanding of events, peoples and changes in the past*

An example taking a building as its focus:

What do we think 'X' might have been thinking when she decided to put her *(castle, factory, house, etc.)* in this place?

What do we think it was like to live or work in?

Who actually built it? How? What tools might they have used?

Why are there towers/turrets/chimneys/windows in these places? What could we see from them when they were first built?

How could we find out the names of the different parts of the building and the materials used?

What might the people in this building have eaten? Where did they get their food?

When it was first built, what sorts of people were living and working in the building? Where might they have come from and what did they all do?

What things were going in and out of this building when it was being used in the past?

Why is this building here? *(e.g. on this hill, by the sea, near this river)*

Why are the windows/doors/gates/chimneys so big/strong/high, etc?

How could we approach this building without being seen?

Where did the people in this building sleep/eat/work/wash/go to the toilet?

What stories can we find out about this building and what stories might it tell?

Other questions about events, people and changes

Look at this picture *(e.g. a Victorian school)*. What has changed least or most since the time of that picture?

How did changes in *(e.g. medicine)* at this time improve different people's lives? of *(e.g. children, soldiers, factory workers)*

What do we think was the most important thing that happened to the village after the opening of the railway?

Why did *(e.g. Boudica, Athenians)* attack the *(e.g. Romans, Spartans)*? What were they hoping to win?

Why were the children evacuated from that town but not from this one? Where would we have sent children from the cities?

How and why did this place change after the war/motorway/canal/factory/plague?

Why do we think 'X' kept on being a Catholic/Protestant in the reign of Queen Elizabeth/Mary, despite all the dangers?

Why did so many children not go to school 100 years ago, even though schools were there for them?

Why was Duke William angry when he heard that Harold had become King of England?

How do we think this artefact would have been made and can we work out how many stages it had in its life?

How many reasons can we think of to explain why Alfred might have hidden from the Danes?

What is different or the same about this street 100 years ago and today?

Can we find any links between these people/places/events? *(from a set of pictures or stories)*

What has changed about children's games between then and now and what has stayed the same?

How does this picture compare to your home? Can you think of reasons why you would like to live here and reasons why you would not?

3 Historical interpretation

Look at the two stories/pictures/letters about *(e.g. World War 2, the Vikings)*. How and where do they disagree with each other?

Which parts of this newspaper story seem 'true' and which are just the opinions of the person who wrote it?

What do we think the artist wanted people to think when he painted this picture?

How does this advert of 50 years ago prove that travelling on roads was easier or harder then?

Do we think the person who wrote this letter was being fair to *(e.g. the owner of the coalmine, the farmer, poor people)*?

Can we think of any reasons why the Bayeux Tapestry may not give a true picture of what actually happened at the Battle of Hastings?

How is the information which the photograph gives different from the extract from the school log book?

How is this story different from that one?

What feelings might people at the time have had about this picture, and how can we find out what they thought?

What has the artist/photographer put in just to make the picture look better?

How realistic do we think this picture is?

4   *Historical enquiry*

Where did people from the time this picture was painted see it? How was this place different from where we are seeing it now?

How do we know whether this picture was posed or natural? What evidence can we see either way?

Why has this (*e.g. carving, poem, building*) survived and come down to us?

What questions would we like to ask the people shown in this piece of evidence?

What are the most important things this piece of evidence can tell us about the people who used it in the past?

How can we find out more than this piece of evidence tells us?

How can we work out whether the Romans made things better or worse for Celts?

If you had to make up a history quiz about this song, what questions would you ask?

Which of these street scenes do we think came first and can we explain why that one is the oldest?

How and why is this an unusual type of (*e.g. hat, food, vehicle, dress, etc*)?

What questions would we ask Mary Seacole if we could meet her?

If we had to choose just one thing to tell people about (*e.g. Ancient Greek jobs, Viking ships, Ancient Egyptian hieroglyphs*) what would it be and why?

An example drawing upon objects:

What do we think this artefact is and was used for?

How can we use this evidence (*e.g. gas mask, poster, diary*) to explain to other people what it must have been like to have been in an air raid?

What can we see that is similar or different about these two artefacts?

Who might have asked for this thing to be made or bought in the first place, and why?

Looking at this picture, can we work out how big was the original?

5   *Organisation and communication*

Who would be most upset or pleased when the law said that children could not work in mines anymore and what might they have thought about it?

From this evidence can we work out three important reasons why so many Victorian children died young?

How can we spot which are the odd ones out in this list of things connected with the Ancient World?

If we had to choose just three words from this list (*of historical terms*) best to describe this picture (*e.g. an historical source*) which ones would they be and why?

How many different ways can we think of to describe the important things going on in this film?

Using these books (*e.g. a pre-supplied set*) can we find at least three places where the word (*e.g. industry, god, legend*) is used? What do these places tell us about what this word means?

Can you draw a picture to show what (*e.g. invasion, court, law*) means in (*e.g. Aztec, Tudor, Victorian*) times, and then explain the picture to us?

The main sentences in this story are jumbled up. Put them back in the order which you think makes the most sense and then compare them with a friend's. How are your new stories different or the same? Which makes most sense, and why?

Which of these artefacts do you think is most important in a house from (*e.g. Tudor, Victorian times*) and why?

In two sentences, what do you think are the two most important things that everyone should know about Benin? Using what everybody else in the class has written, write a list of 'five little-known facts about Benin'.

Write as detailed a description as you can of the most important thing you saw on the visit. How many different things can it tell us about life in the past?

Can you tell us three important things you have learnt during this term's history topic and one thing you would have liked to have known more about?

Draw a flow diagram showing us how you are using (*e.g. the Internet, books, TV, pictures, artefacts*) to answer questions about our topic. Which have been the most and least useful things to use?

This picture shows two people from (*e.g. Ancient Greece, Victorian Britain*). Can you fill in the speech bubbles to show:

- something they might be arguing about?
- a new discovery or big event they could just have heard of?
- what they might be saying about their night out?
- comments about each others' clothes?
- what they might be talking about if they worked together?

6   Teaching History in Practice

A. Writing Through History

Because history draws upon many kinds of text through its questions, it can play a crucial role in developing children's literacy. Talking about, reading and writing historical texts in the following ways enriches English, literacy and history, fitting with national curriculum English requirements and the National Literacy Strategy and Framework. They are especially useful for promoting historical interpretations, enquiry and communication. Nearly all can be word-processed as easily as hand-written.

This document touches upon the following underlying questions:

- *How do history curricula advance multimedia or only written literacy skills?*
- *Whether history learning is only communicated through writing or is expressed via other media;*
- *The extent to which communities understand history as school work or lifelong knowledge.*

Multimedia and literacy skills

- **Copying text** only alongside discussion and with a conceptual purpose. Can children match words copied to historical pictures? Can learners use the words copied to tell back a story about the past? Can learners put objects and associated words into chronological order?
- **Labelling and captioning** e.g. parts of historical pictures, timelines, classroom displays, models.
- **Completing** e.g. sentences, paragraphs or pages with historical phrases centred around important historical question or command words such as: *Who, how, what, where, why, when, in what order, which, if, whether, did, can, try, find, search, could, might, research, enquire, should, choose, because, since, compare, think, remember, tell, explain, show, list, order.*
- **Choosing, sorting and listing** e.g. historical characters, events, causes, types of evidence, suited to activities on cards or screen.
- **Describing** e.g. an historical event, room, reason why, result, point of view: starting with words and lists progressing to sentences and paragraphs.

- **Explaining** e.g. what an historical object is and where it comes from, the life story of an historical person or place.
- **Questioning** e.g. an historical 'eyewitness', a significant leader, the teacher hot-seated, objects, pictures, other children.
- **Creating imaginatively** e.g. imagining the past through a list, phrase, haiku, song, poem, news report, conversation, advert or riddle.
- **Creating transactionally** e.g. in an historical setting creating a formal message, notice, invitation, instruction, law, judgement.
- **Editing** e.g. from historical texts such as interviews, newspapers, inventories, gravestones: editing to find an answer to an historical question or support a discussion.
- **Reporting** e.g. on an historical visit or enquiry, on groupwork, in journalistic style on an historical 'event'.
- **Processing** e.g. children describing different stages in a building's past, using a flow chart to explain how they have researched an historical topic, using a timeline or cards to explain their own historical knowledge,
- **Note taking** e.g. from historical books, videos, talks, CD ROMs or websites. Presentation, recall, research and a few key words are vital.
- **Narrating for a scribe** e.g. an historically descriptive letter, diary, information, time-line, argument or description.
- **Summarising** e.g. historical similarities/differences, a judgement, experiences, learning as diagrams, charts, key words, sentences or prose.
- **Telling and retelling** e.g. events from children's own lives such as special days or holidays, or an historical story children have heard, read, seen or researched themselves.
- **Dramatising** e.g. discussing, devising, acting historical interpretations and episodes. Then writing these up using: key words, significant phrases, points of view about a particular turning point, a summary, a script.
- **Persuading** others in an historical setting e.g. what a 'new' museum gallery should show, which objects to choose from the collections to go in its displays, how it should be advertised.
- **Discussing and arguing** e.g. advocacy for/against an historical character, action, change or judgement; reconciling how the 'same' historical event is seen by different people in different ways.
- **Mimicking 'in the style of . . .'** e.g. children devise guide books, museum information boards, historical stories, old songs.
- **Forging** e.g. a passport, a poem, a form, a journal, a newspaper, an essay.

B. Learning by Looking: Visual Evidence in History

This collection of advice and teaching ideas has accumulated over the last decade, reflecting a desire to make history curriculum materials as accessible and multimedia as possible. This document is especially useful in considering the following underlying questions:

- *Does history learning develop multiple or singular intelligences?*

- *Are history curricula inter-disciplinary or subject-specific?*
- *Should history learning only be communicated through writing or expressed via other media?*

Curriculum background

National curriculum history asks teachers to support learning with a 'range of sources of information' (DfEE 1999a pp. 16–20) including visual sources. Ideas such as *interpretation, representation and evaluation* are also central to national curriculum subjects such as English or art and design: learning by looking cuts across subjects.

Most children can use pictures as evidence, making them invaluable for group activities. Pictures can also stretch higher attainers: the reward for being bright and hard working should not always be more reading and writing. Sets of postcards, available at most museums, lend themselves well to targeted small group work.

History can be learnt about in 2D and 3D forms: drawn, painted, printed, photographed, filmed, sewn, carved etc. The most common representations children experience are *photographs and film*. These often represent other visual forms such as paintings, statues or posters. Because photographs and film are ubiquitous it is vital that children learn about them in history. Equally, since children only sporadically experience forms such as sculpture or mural 'in the original', history offers many visual learning opportunities on site visits.

Thinking historical and artistically means questioning the *purposes* of a picture or piece. Was it conceived and has it survived because of decorative, commercial, newsworthy, commemorative, persuasive, creative or emotive qualities? This links with audience. Where would the piece have been seen and by whom?

Developing *interpretative skills* is central to history and 'learning by looking'. Because visual images are set, framed or bounded in some way, encourage children to think about what was left out, and why. Similarly, most pictures or photographs are posed: how does this affect them as evidence? How else could an image have been presented?

Classroom foreground

The following visually-led activities support most aspects of historical 'knowledge, skills and understanding':

1   In general:

- Spend enough time. A picture is worth a thousand words, or about three sides of closely written A4. Look long and hard at just one picture. Concentrate first on describing in detail what we see with our eyes, before thinking about what it 'means' for history.
- Having done this, compare any particular historical picture with others similar in subject or style.

- Ask children to research other texts to find and explain their own comparisons.
- Children or teacher put pictures into groups according to different criteria and ask questions about them.
- Make a class picture corner or gallery on a particular period or event, with dated and explanatory labels.
- Use and show specialist vocabulary to help children think more exactly about visual images (e.g. portrait, frame, poster, advert, style, commission, perspective, etc).

2   Discuss in detail aspects of a particular picture or image:

- What is in its foreground and background?
- Do most pictures have a focus such as a person, object or event? What is it in this example and why?
- Can we explain what this picture might mean to different people such as its painter or photographer, owner, participant, etc?
- When was this image made and why was it made in this way?
- What does this picture mean to us now, what could it have meant when it was made and how did the artist make it meaningful?

Talk, structured in this way, will help children to analyse pictures and understand that images are manufactured, not natural.

3   Teaching activities with historical images should have specific and meaningful purposes. For example:

- Children researching and assuming an 'in-role' identity adopted from the picture.
- Devising questions to ask and imagined answers to offer from historical subjects or artists.
- Covering part of the picture to focus thinking upon what is showing and speculation about what is covered.
- Adopting a striptease approach, logging how interpretations of a visual image alter as more is revealed.
- Imagining being given this visual image originally, or being in it. What does it tell us about the past?
- Choosing two pictures from a set of five according to criteria and ideas relevant to history e.g. usefulness for a particular enquiry, propaganda purposes, commemorative potential, as sources for quiz questions;
- Giving an historical image a new title or a label in a museum to help viewers learn history from it.

Historically educational things to do with photographs

Children need access to a range of visual images: photographs are *one*, not *the* visual image. Having said that, photographs will be the commonnest visual resource in most classrooms. The following teaching activities concentrate upon using photographs to develop historical knowledge, skills and understanding across the range of requirements for national curriculum history. Most can be used with or adapted for children aged 4–14.

Background preparation

1   Collect images on a single historical theme to show that they represent diverse points of view and opinions, rather than a simple record or self-evident truth.
2   Discuss 'sets' of visual images on historical themes such as family albums, school log books, photo journalism or fiction, travel brochures, estate agents' details, education packs or textbooks. How do the images in each set differ?
3   Encourage children to take and bring in their own photographs of historical remains such as buildings, landscapes, sites or features. Site visit or holiday snaps often contain these sorts of historical reference and can be used for enquiry, comparison and discussion on purpose, style, composition, etc.
4   As an independent task ask children to look for visual images relating to periods or events. Different sources such as newspapers, catalogues, the Internet, travel brochures, photo albums or books will be useful for different periods, such as Ancient Greece or nineteenth century Britain. A class collection can be analysed into different types of image.
5   Teachers and/or children can provide provenance for photographs, particularly local ones: and maps or a drawing to show where a photograph was taken from, information about when, who, why it was taken.
6   A set of images or photographs can be a stimulating, accessible introduction to an historical study or period. Images offer starting points for devising enquiry questions on themes shown such as people, landscapes, beliefs, stories, maps, language, foods or products. Children can research using books and ICT to back up what a collection of images tells us about a period or people.
7   Ask teacher-led historical questions about a photograph to model questions for children. What sorts of people or place are shown, where and when do you think it is, what different objects or materials can you see, what sort of settlement is this, etc?

Foreground activities

8   Individually or in pairs, children devise historical questions for people in photographs and experiment with answers they might give.
9   As above, learners use bubble writing to speculate about what people in a photograph might be seeing/thinking/wishing/feeling at that moment.
10   Students devise explanatory captions or titles for singles, groups or sets of photographs such as 'this evidence suggests that . . .' or 'this image is important because . . . .'
11   Children use writing on sticky pads to describe and label the main historical information and features of a photograph, and ask questions about aspects that are unclear or invite speculation.

12 For a thematic set of pictures students isolate and count variables: women and men, adults and children, natural or posed, with or without text. How would this compare to now or another time? What does this tell us about the time, place or photographer?

13 The teacher mounts a picture on paper, leaving a wide border. Children write questions and explanations of what they see around the border. They view each other's work, criticise the explanations and try to answer the questions.

14 Students sort pictures into sets: images with/without people or machines, those showing children or not, those useful for enquiries about jobs, houses, clothes, etc., in the past.

15 Ask a child to choose a photograph or image from an historical set that most relates to or contrasts with their own life. Can they explain why?

16 Students imagine the sounds and the smells that might accompany this picture in real life. How many are there, and how do they compare to here and now?

17 Children rank pictures in order or choose two extremes from a set of photographs according to different criteria: rich to poor, typical to unusual, attractive to ugly, female to male, new to old, natural to posed, simple to advanced, rural to urban, etc. How can they explain their choices?

18 Give different groups of children different pictures taken from a larger set. Ask them to record their assumptions about the time, people, place from this sample. Then give all children access to the whole set and ask for similar assumptions to be made. Put all the photographs and assumptions on display to ask whether assumptions changed or were sound as more evidence was revealed.

19 Look for similarities and differences between past scenes shown in a set of historical images and the world in which students live (e.g. buildings, landscape, dress, appearance, wealth, services, technology, etc.).

20 Following reading and research, children choose just five photos for a pack. This will show a child of their age from another country what life was like in the historical period or place in question. These can be photocopied and supporting texts written by children.

21 Ask students to 'crop' a large historical picture and then show it to other students. They are asked to analyse and make assumptions before being allowed to see the whole picture and repeat the process. Compare assumptions before and after access to the whole.

22 Towards the end of a study and using an informative historical image, ask children to write from it: a diary entry, a newspaper report, a description of the scene in a letter, a poem, a criticism of the photograph's accuracy, a reaction by the person shown, a museum label or book caption. This supports the difficult task of accurate but empathetic writing.

23 Choosing just one person in a photograph students write 'a day in their life', using other historical sources as accompaniment.

24 Design and frame a contemporary photograph which is similar in content to a chosen historical example e.g. a family in their front room, children in the street, modes of transport, ordinary houses. Ask children to make, display and explain comparisons.

25 For a particular, action-led historical image discuss and design 'what happened next' or 'what happened before this'. An image, text or dramatic reconstruction can communicate conclusions.

26 Ask children to discuss what they can see 'signs of' in an historical picture, but is not actually shown (e.g. feelings such as fear or love, other people beyond the scene depicted, the climate).

27 Students imagine and then speak or write the words of the photographer or painter as she explained: what she wanted from the photograph, how she wanted the people arranged in it, what she wanted to show etc. How would she present it to the person who commissioned the image, or the people in it? (Figure 6.1).

Figure 6.1 Interpreting art in the context of historical enquiry

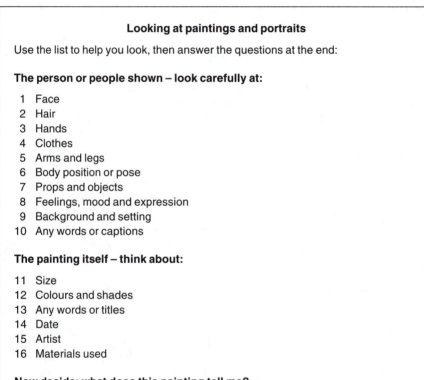

Looking at paintings and portraits

Use the list to help you look, then answer the questions at the end:

The person or people shown – look carefully at:

1   Face
2   Hair
3   Hands
4   Clothes
5   Arms and legs
6   Body position or pose
7   Props and objects
8   Feelings, mood and expression
9   Background and setting
10 Any words or captions

The painting itself – think about:

11 Size
12 Colours and shades
13 Any words or titles
14 Date
15 Artist
16 Materials used

Now decide: what does this painting tell me?

a   I think the title of this painting should be . . .
b   The person in the picture seems to be saying . . .
c   The artist wanted to . . .
d   I think this picture was painted because . . .
e   This picture makes me feel . . .
f   I have spotted . . .
g   I would like to ask . . .
h   From this picture I have found out that . . .

C. Quality Teaching in Primary History?

These two sheets were developed from work by Felicity Golding, an adviser with Norfolk LEA (Figure 6.2). They are designed to support history curriculum leaders in their monitoring and evaluation. Although there are many other monitoring criteria or themes (see Bage 1997), the school's history policy statement being the most obvious, the brevity of this framework makes it especially useful for considering the following underlying questions in this book:

- *Is history teaching perceived as technical delivery or moral art?*
- *Does history teaching standardise or differentiate pedagogy and materials?*
- *Should history teaching promote transmission or analysis of historical knowledge?*

Figure 6.2 *Monitoring and supporting history teaching and learning*

Things to look for when monitoring history teaching	Observation	Indirect
1 A variety of organisational strategies is used to include: individual and paired tasks/cooperative group work/whole class lesson/ discussion/ story-telling.		
2 There is an absence of copied or dictated work and a presence of teacher enthusiasm.		
3 Experiential learning through visits, fieldwork in built or natural environments and imaginative or dramatic reconstructions appear in planning.		
4 A wide range of historical sources is available and used: e.g. books, newspapers and other documents, oral history, maps, photographs, pictures, film, music, artefacts, ICT.		
5 Resources are stimulating, appropriate to age and abilities of children and sensitive to issues of equal opportunity and multicultural education.		
6 Teachers support pupils in selecting, using and evaluating sources, not merely as illustration.		
7 Teachers encourage children to frame their own questions and enquiries and teach them how to.		
8 The lesson is planned as part of a sequence of lessons that fit into an agreed, used scheme of work.		
9 Assessments are specific enough to support children's progress in historical learning.		

Things to look for when monitoring history learning	Observation	Indirect
1 Children are motivated and involved.		
2 Children are provided with challenging but attainable historical tasks.		
3 Children acquire historical information.		
4 Children ask and answer historical questions.		
5 Children analyse and compare different sources.		
6 Children can investigage historical topics.		
7 There are opportunities to communicate learning orally, visually, through drama and in writing using a range of techniques.		
8 Children can explain possible reasons for learning about history.		
9 Children can evaluate their own work.		
10 Children can explain connections between history and other subjects.		
11 Children can recognise cross-curricular themes and spiritual, moral, social and cultural issues in history lessons, and vice versa. For example children's attitudes might show: • curiosity • a sense of respect for the past • how the past has helped shape the present • respect for evidence • tolerance of a range of opinions		

D. Assessing History

Although this book is published after a decade of an English national history curriculum, assessing younger children's learning in history remains in its infancy. The precision of history assessment through examinations across the 14–21 age range, derived from decades of experience, has yet to be replicated for younger learners. Without considerable investment in research and development it may never arrive. Until that happens the few research projects in the area (e.g. Lee, Ashby and Dickinson 1996) and syntheses of practice may be our best guides.

The following document attempts both (see Figure 6.3). It is useful in considering this book's following underlying questions:

- *Does history learning start from the curriculum's requirements or children's needs?*
- *Is history only communicated through writing or expressed via other media?*
- *Does history aim for knowledge through questioning or memorisation?*

Figure 6.3 Assessing younger children's learning in history

Some premises for history assessment

1 Complex teacher-assessment systems in history are unsustainable, even in large secondary schools with specialist departments.
2 History is recursive rather than linear, making level-dominated and numerically expressed assessments difficult at best and irrelevant at worst.
3 The 'Knowledge, skills and understanding' aspects of NC History in the Programme of Study connect to the NC History Level Descriptions, but not in a clear or instantly accessible way.
4 *Assessment* is not a blanket term for a set of common practices: *fitness for purpose* is a more powerful idea. Formative or summative, quantitative or qualitative, public or private, spontaneous or anticipated, closed or open, spoken or written, individual or grouped, information or ideas-led: these history assessments all have a place. A useful way of refining assessment is to consider *how can I use it to inform children's learning, teachers' teaching, and links with home or school improvement?* Unless such benefits are visible assessment may be pointless.
5 History assessment needs to fit into whole-school policies on assessment.

Formative assessment in history

1 The acronym *QUILL* focuses formative history assessments. *QUILL* implies teachers teaching and talking with children about their grasp of:

QU Questions (Historical enquiry, organisation and communication)
I   Information (breadth of study, knowledge and understanding of events, people and changes in the past, organisation and communication) and *Ideas* (especially chronological understanding, historical interpretation and enquiry)
LL Language Learning (throughout)

(a) Historical *Questions* of evidence e.g.

using key or command words like 'who, how, what, where, why, when, in what order, which, if, whether, did, can, try, find, search, could, might, research, enquire, should, choose, because, since, compare, think, remember, tell, explain, show, list, order, imagine, what if, what else'

using evidence like documents, printed sources, artefacts, pictures and photographs, music, buildings and sites, people, books, computers.

(b) Historical *Information* e.g.

how meaningful are the historical stories or accounts from different studies to children at KS1?

can KS2 children explain why the ideas or beliefs of a people are characteristic of that time?

can KS3 children explain how gender, class, culture, beliefs and ethnicity give rise to historically diverse experiences across different peoples studied?

(c) Historical *Ideas* or concepts e.g.

sequences, events, periods, accounts, changes, reasons, results, differences, similarities, interpretations, representations, enquiry, research.

(d) Historical and literacy-led *Language Learning* e.g.

Learning how to use the above words or equivalents plus terms like ancient, modern, BC, AD, century and decade.

Learning how to use dates, specialist terms and names from different studies in historical speech, reading and writing.

Learning how to communicate historically through descriptions, structured narratives and explanations.

2 History in schools is not confined to the history section of the national curriculum: much of historical value is also reflected in the 'values, aims and purposes' of the national curriculum (DfEE 1999b pp. 10–13) or in school policy statements. For instance, when we teach history we teach not just cognition, but about affection and values. We show in our actions how we cherish curiosity: we nurture a sense of identities, we foster tolerance, we scrutinise but develop respect for the past, we promote the use of imagination. We try to demonstrate how to use scepticism, how to link past and present, how to examine ethics. We work together on sharpening our senses of plurality and common humanity: we may even imbue our learners with a burning desire to make meaning of the contradictory worlds they will inhabit.

Although numerical quantification cannot describe such personal qualities, this does not mean their development should pass unassessed or uncommented. OFSTED has long since had to report upon the *spiritual, moral, social and cultural development of pupils* in schools (OFSTED 1995 p. 47). History can make major contributions to all of these areas.

Summative assessment in history (the child speaks)

My teacher is not going to tick me into a thousand boxes, and end up early in one herself. Instead she will use professional knowledge and judgement to make me better at history, using stepped bureaucratic levels only where they can feed back into my unpredictable and expanding mind.

She must report on my history at the end of each key stage (see DfEE 1999a) by judging which level in the attainment target best fits my performance . I hope she will do this by concentrating on verbs – on what I can *do*.

To help her I have broken down the fat paragraphs in the history attainment target into thinner, *I CAN DO* statements. I need not achieve all of these to be awarded a level: they are there to help my teacher articulate her view of my general level of achievement.

She will spot that most of the sentences below combine my mastery of historical questions, information, ideas and language learning (QUILL). She will remember that I often spend a year or two working on or within a level, or dotting between levels, rather than neatly climbing to the next step. Being a confident and critical professional, she can handle planning from the different elements of the programme of study and from the 'values, aims and purposes' of the school or national curriculum, at the same time as using these rather inadequate 'levels' to sketch my progress.

So, teacher: which one of the following levels *best fits my performance in history*, derived as these are from the levels in the attainment target of national curriculum history? (see Figures 6.4 and 6.5).

Figure 6.4 Positive formative assessment: I can do . . .

I can do history? Positive formative assessment

1   *I have achieved Level 1 in NC history because I can:*
    (a) Distinguish between past and present in my own and other people's lives;
    (b) Sequence some historical events and objects;
    (c) Use everyday terms about the passing of time;
    (d) Recount episodes from stories about the past;
    (e) Use information to find some answers to questions about the past.

2   *I have achieved Level 2 in NC history because I can:*
    (a) Use words about the passing of time to order events and objects;
    (b) Distinguish between aspects of my life and aspects of life in the past;
    (c) Show what I know about people and events from a time beyond living memory;
    (d) Suggest some reasons why people in the past might have acted as they did;
    (e) Show some ways in which the past is represented;
    (f) Answer questions about the past by observing sources of information.

3   *I have achieved Level 3 in NC history because I can:*
    (a) Show that I know that history splits the past into different periods;
    (b) Recognise some similarities and differences between these different periods;
    (c) Use dates and terms whilst explaining history;
    (d) Show knowledge and understanding of some important events, peoples and changes studied in history lessons;
    (e) Suggest a few reasons and results for events and changes;
    (f) Show that I know that the past is represented in different ways;
    (g) Move beyond simple observations when using information sources to answer questions about the past.

4   *I have achieved Level 4 in NC history because I can:*
    (a) Show that I know and understand some British and world history;
    (b) Describe some main events, peoples and changes learnt about;
    (c) Use my knowledge to describe characteristic features and changes within and across periods of history;
    (d) Give some reasons and results for main events and changes;
    (e) Show how aspects of the past have been represented and interpreted in different ways;

(f) Select and combine information from sources;

(g) Begin to produce structured work using dates and terms;

5 *I have achieved Level 5 in NC history because I can:*

(a) Show increasing depth of knowledge and understanding of British and world history;

(b) Use my knowledge to describe and link features of past societies and periods;

(c) Describe events, peoples and changes and use that knowledge to offer reasons and results;

(d) Understand that some events, people and changes have been interpreted differently and suggest reasons why;

(e) Use my knowledge to begin to evaluate information from sources and identify sources useful for particular tasks;

(f) Select and organise information to produce structured work using dates and terms.

6 *I have achieved Level 6 in NC history because I can:*

(a) Use my knowledge of British and world history to link things within and beyond past societies and periods;

(b) Examine and explain the reasons and results of changes;

(c) Describe and start to analyse different historical interpretations;

(d) Identify and evaluate information sources to reach or support conclusions;

(e) Select, deploy and organise information to produce structured work including dates and historical terms.

Figure 6.5 Some history assessment tasks

Some history assessment tasks

This section abbreviates ideas for assessing children's learning across Levels 1–4 of the national curriculum history attainment target.

For Levels 1 and 2

1 A piece of paper is divided into 4 or 6. Child retells and sequences a history story in words or pictures.

2 Photocopies of key pages or incidents from a history book or story are given to children to put back into order and explain.

3 From cards with pictures but without writing, children re-tell a history story. The pictures can be of historical people, places or objects.

4 Puppets, pictures or cut-outs of people are used for sequencing and the asking and answering of historical questions.

5 Objects from history can achieve the same. Try sets, for instance: charcoal, quill pen, pencil, fountain pen and biro; Roman oil lamp, candle, paraffin lamp, electric light.

6 At the class timeline or display children explain: what is there that is different or the same from nowadays?

7   Children draw and talk about a series of pictures showing 'Then and Now' comparing specific things such as toys, clothes, weapons, transport, etc.

8   On a sheet with pictures of past and present features, children identify which are from past and present.

9   Have a 'then and now' page divided into a column for each period children have knowledge of (e.g. 'Now, Early People, Castles, Grandparents' for KS1). Can children describe the differences or similarities and explain them?

10 Children observe a mystery object. What do they think it is? How might it have been used? After discussion children draw a reconstruction of the object being used. Can they explain their picture historically?

11 From an historical picture or photo, children choose an object or person to express through mime. They can be 'paused' by the watchers and asked questions about themselves: use the questions and answers as assessment materials.

12 Children list or have listed for them single response words to an object or picture e.g. 'rusty, valuable, old'. To achieve Level 2: can they turn these words into historical questions?

13 Ask children to pose questions starting with 'how' or 'why' about an historical object or picture. Other children try to answer them.

14 Children are given a piece of historical evidence (e.g. artefact, picture) and asked to write a book caption, museum notice or label explaining what this evidence tells you about the people who made or used it.

For Levels 3 and 4

1   From a series of sources (books, pictures, objects etc.) used in a topic, children pick 'the most useful' and explain what they have learnt from it.

2   Ask children to pick a person from their history topic who they like, disliked, wanted to be, was the most important etc. Can they explain why?

3   At the timeline: Why do you think . . . did that? Why might . . . have lived like that? Why do you think this person is . . . in that picture? Why did the . . . build in that way? Why did the . . . invade, settle, fight, travel, farm, bury people differently from us? Teachers and children devise and answer historical questions.

4   Provide an outline drawing of a modern child and a character from history, each with a speech bubble. Either let the child decide on the question and let her fill in both speech bubbles. Alternatively teacher and children decide on the question and the child just completes the character's 'answer'.

5   Children place previous history titles or icons (e.g. the parthenon, Roman wall, Sutton Hoo Helmet, Viking long boat, carriages or cars, local school etc.) on the class timeline. Having located and identifed different studies they answer questions about them as above.

6   A part of a document is given to children, the rest having been torn, burnt or smudged. What can the fragment tell us about life in the past?

7   Give children an historical question and some different sources with which to answer it (e.g. picture, artefact, document, visit). Can they write an account drawing these sources together? Can they devise and answer their own question from a batch of sources?

8   Give children a batch of different sources such as music, picture, artefact, document or visit. Can they write a caption for a museum display drawing these sources together? Can they devise and answer questions from the batch of sources which might make the display more interesting?

9 Give children a batch of different sources on the same study as above. Can they order these for one or more of the following criteria: usefulness, reliability, scarcity, fairness? Can they explain their order?

10 Using specialist historical vocabulary printed on cards (e.g. invasion, slavery, trade, evidence, beliefs) ask children to remember or research examples from history studied so far. Cards are then matched to books, pictures, artefacts etc. and children explain their understanding of the term.

11. Children are asked to describe 'important' things about a particular period or people studied. They can research this, but to prevent copying of chunks take books away at point of telling or writing.

12. Children are given the first, prompting sentences of paragraphs to complete e.g. 'The Ancient Greeks were special because' 'The Victorians thought differently in the following ways' 'Lots of things have changed around here such as'.

7 History Curriculum in Practice

I. History and Literacy

This can be used as a resource for thinking about history and the national literacy strategy' (sections A and B) and some linguistically-led issues concerning history within the broader, new national curriculum (section C). The document touches upon this book's underlying questions:

- *Are history curricula negotiated teacher to child or standardised?*
- *Do they advance multimedia or only written literacy skills?*
- *Are they inter-disciplinary or subject specific?*
- *Does history learning develop multiple or singular intelligences?*
- *Does history teaching challenge or implement a school's stated aims for learning history?*
- *Does history teaching emphasise personal interpretations or social control?*

A. Curriculum planning and timetabling

In theory, the National Literacy Strategy Framework for Key Stages 1 and 2 (hereafter NLSF) provides many opportunities for inter-disciplinary work:

> Where appropriate, literacy teaching should be linked to work in other areas of the curriculum. For example, during the Literacy Hour pupils might be searching and retrieving from information texts used in science, writing instructions linked to a technology topic, studying myths, autobiographies or stories linked to a study unit in history.
>
> (DfEE 1998 p. 13)

In practice the introduction of literacy and numeracy hours has narrowed the curriculum in primary schools, many of whom now timetable subjects such as history in short, afternoon blocks of perhaps two half hours per week. Content-rich, concept-led disciplines such as history, science and geography are ill-suited to this approach and a more pragmatic 'mixed economy' of curriculum planning may help. For instance, history can be linked to some NLSF requirements through the use of historical materials. Following on from 'literacy mornings' history can be taught during 'afternoons' as a distinct subject, every term, perhaps for three weeks. Such history-led but still inter-disciplinary enquiries can take their place alongside those emphasising science, geography or art and design.

B. NLSF 'Range' and 'Level'

The NLSF is structured around three levels of work: word, sentence and text. The 'skills' attached to word and sentence level tasks rely on teachers employing the rich range of texts the NLSF prescribes, and developing teaching strategies to motivate children to engage with them. History offers a plentiful range of both. As a discipline it is centrally concerned with reading evidence for information and understanding. When taught well it is also intrinsically interesting and enjoyable. History offers especially rich language materials and tasks perhaps because it straddles the worlds of fiction and non-fiction. For instance history is *fictionally-influenced*. By definition history concerns things that happened in the past. These realities are now gone and therefore require imaginative reconstruction in historians' minds. The results are often communicated in narrative or narrative-led forms, telling a story over time as it seems to an author. Yet in *factual* terms, most of the events historians study really did happen and are as empirically demonstrable as the laws of gravity, or the value of pi. Historians mostly aspire to be analytically accurate, to reveal their sources for scholastic scrutiny and to write rigorously tested accounts as 'true' as *reliable non-fiction*.

The NLSF is simplistic in its modelling of the relationships between fiction and non-fiction but does offer a host of interesting history possibilities. For instance, what follows are teaching ideas mixing handling of artefacts, literacy, history and the telling of fictional and non-fictional stories (Figure 7.1).

Figure 7.1 History, artefacts and storytelling

History, artefacts and storytelling in the literacy hour

Historical artefacts and told stories can be used as a teaching resource to support the objectives of the National Literacy Strategy Framework for KS1 and KS2 at word, sentence and text level:

- storytelling (fiction and non-fiction) suffuses the NLSF (see also Bage 1999a pp.153–61);
- handling objects motivates some children more than text;
- objects have their own stories to tell and their own texts to be read;
- 'original' objects are unique in ways that mass-produced reproductions or big books are not.

Two sections of the hour lend themselves to this:

- Whole Class Storytelling Activities focusing on Shared Reading or Writing.

- Guided Group and Independent Work focusing on Guided Reading, Guided Writing and Independent Work.

The following teaching ideas can be adapted for use in any of these.

1   Oral History (e.g. NLSF Non-fiction Y6 term 1)
Children prepare questions and interview respondents. Important stages which can be broken down either into Literacy Hour whole class activities or group work are:

- practising interview skills
- securing interviewees
- deciding questions
- choosing recording and reference methods
- analysing the evidence collected
- comparing evidence
- drawing conclusions
- framing further questions relating to other historical evidence
- communicating results
- thanking participants.

Memory-jogging starting points for oral history and local stories include a range of objects and evidence: antiques, souvenirs, memorabilia, family treasures, local maps, favourite walks, photographs, printed or spoken stories, buildings, scars, toys, food, clothes or key national events.

2   Storyboxes or Bags (e.g. NLSF Fiction and Poetry Y3 terms 1, 2)
After pulling them from a box or bag children describe artefacts or representations of historical evidence to a small group (e.g. a Viking bag and artefacts, Victorian penny, book, school photograph, reproduction toy). They then devise written or spoken stories and/or poems about them. Variations include:

- using models of artefacts or figures;
- asking children to make their own storyboxes;
- impromptu stories based on drawing objects singly out of a bag;
- giving children the same sets and comparing resultant stories;
- devising toy museums including layout, signs, audio-visual effects etc.

3   Storyboarding, Storymapping and Illustrating (e.g. NLSF Non-fiction Year 4 terms 1, 2)
Ask children to tell the story of an object, or collection of objects, into sequences of pictures. *Storyboarding* does this by imagining the stories as a series of scenes, sketched in rough form with matchstick figures and simple labels. *Storymapping* similarly uses pictures and arrows to explain relationships between the elements of a story, but without necessarily boxing them in chronological order. *Illustrating* can vary from children retelling a heard story by drawing in a number of boxes through to complex series' of cartoons, murals or tapestries. All these techniques help learners to translate a story from one genre into another and can be used in Non-Fiction as well as Fiction.

4 A Storied Production (e.g. NLSF Non-fiction Y3 term 1)

The story of an object is told through the actions or materials needed to produce, transport, sell, use and preserve it. A witnessed example from Frances Sword (Fitzwilliam Museum, Cambridge see Bage 1999a) took the following stages in the life of a Greek vase, during which children questioned, demonstrated, mimed or listened to the story:

- digging clay by slaves
- the potter and wheel
- firing and fuel
- transport-by-pack-animal
- the agora
- the purchaser and purchaser's house
- the vase's final resting place, and why
- archaeologist
- museum conservators and visitors

The author has successfully used the same principle for modern examples e.g. Victorian bricks, World War 2 bombs.

5 Talking Objects (e.g. NLSF Fiction Y3 term 2)

Similarly a real or imagined object is 'brought' to a circle. Its stages are described and explained individually or co-operatively. Questions are asked about the object's owners, life, purpose and experiences (e.g. Roman oil lamp, Tudor hornbook).

- making;
- using;
- losing;
- leaving;
- finding;
- stealing or preserving . . .

6 An Expert with Objects (e.g. NLSF Non-fiction Y1 terms 1, 2)

In this tasks are set up which allow children to practise and grow into 'experts'. Adopting roles such as archaeologist, museum manager, documentary maker, teacher, journalist, conservator or antique dealer children are asked to:

- Enact a specific job e.g. 'You are an archaeologist. The phone rings with news of an exciting find. What do you pack in your bag?'
- Approach a piece or collection of evidence to solve an historical problem e.g. 'How would you turn these pictures and objects into an interesting museum display?'
- Report on an interesting case e.g. 'How would you write up finding a rare painting in an attic for the local newspaper?'

7 Statues and Paintings (e.g. NLSF Fiction and Non-fiction, Y5 term 3)

After looking at commemorative art (e.g. statues, figures, plaques, paintings, stained glass etc from secular and religious communities) choose an historical character or event to research and commemorate. Divide the class into 'statues' and 'sculptors', 'painters' and 'models' or more ambitiously, 'dancers' and choreographers', with the latter arranging the former for two minutes. All works are viewed and can be questioned. Captions/plaques can be written. Children experience both roles. This focuses thinking and language on interpretations and representations of history.

8   Role Play and Artefacts (e.g. NLSF Fiction Y1 term 2)

Numerous role play possibilities exist with objects. Single artefacts or collections can be handled and discussed by children before a role play and can suggest story-lines or 'frozen pictures' for children to design and perform. But a key to success in the role play is that *it has to be rehearsed and performed without touching the object*. This means that children get the best of both worlds. They handle and learn from the object (in discussion) but then have to represent it in movement, mime, dialogue etc. If you do allow a 'prop' into a role-play, it often becomes the centre of attention and children struggle for its possession.

9   Any questions? (e.g. NLSF Non-fiction Y4 terms 2, 3)

Having been given objects, children prepare to interview their 'former owners' about them. Questions are prepared, ordered and compared. With a collection of objects about the same period or person, a familiar format (e.g. news, chat show, maga-zine) can be used and children or teacher may 'answer' questions in-role.

10   Talking Objects Through (e.g. NLSF Non-fiction Y3 terms 1, 2, 3)

- From sets of evidence including objects and/or pictures, decide on the everyday jobs that needed doing around a Tudor or Victorian house. If your group was a family unit or work gang, who would do what? Write a list of jobs imagining you were going away for a week.
- As managers of a Greek or Egyptian museum you have been given pictures of objects that were dug up in your country then taken to Britain. Work out which three to demand back, and how to support your case in a letter or broadcast.
- Learners design, describe, explain or justify a classroom display or museum including artefacts, pictures of artefacts and explanations of artefacts (e.g. *From Romans to Vikings* or *The Story of Writing*). Explanatory texts and labels connect these. Questions about the resultant story are asked and recorded.

C. Twelve checkpoints for co-ordinating language and history

This section is designed to help history, English and special educational needs co-ordinators work together in ways recommended by the national curriculum's 'General Teaching Requirements', particularly those relating to language. Many schools' existing planning and practice builds upon the national curriculum's 'Use of language across the curriculum' requirements about writing, speaking, listening and reading. The following twelve questions develop these:

1 *Are our assessments specific enough to help learners understand how to improve their abilities to use language historically and accurately?*

For instance NC history *level descriptions* are suffused with linguistic requirements. At Level 2 pupils are 'using terms connected with the passing of time', at Level 4 'they describe some of the main events, people and changes' of different periods and at Level 7, produce 'well structured narratives, descriptions and explanations' (DfEE 1999c 'About the attainment targets' p. 29).

2 *Does the language of lessons and the history scheme of work make real the aims of the school?*

Teachers translate programmes of study into *schemes of work* and *individual lessons* and decide how to use level descriptions to support assessment. This planning should relate to the wider curriculum aims of the school which often mention literacy, oracy, communication and confidence, as well as civic ideals. These all rest upon language. For instance, a school policy promoting understanding of democracy, citizenship or tolerance logically has to teach pupils what these terms mean in history.

3 *Does children's learning in history exemplify whole-school language policies?*

Most schools have whole-school policies for English, special educational needs, teaching English as a second or additional language, assessment, equal opportunities, multicultural education, etc. Discussing history and the use of language across the curriculum is a part of these. History is a practice ground for English as well as a discipline in its own right, providing another and motivating context within which pupils can speak, listen and read.

4 *Do we teach how to use language as an historical source, as well as a tool?*

Language is also a practice ground for history, since words are an historical source as well as necessity. As an eminent author says in a novel 'we open our mouths and out flow words whose ancestries we do not even know . . . in a single sentence of idle chatter we preserve Latin, Anglo-Saxon, Norse . . .' (Lively 1987 p. 41). Anglicised words from the wider world could be added, immortalising the multi-cultural experience upon which English (and British) culture and history rest.

5 *Do history lessons and resources build upon concepts and words explored in other subjects?*

For instance, expressing chronology in language rather than number makes understandings of 'time' more accessible to most students. This is reinforced in national curriculum history's 'knowledge, skills and understanding' about chronology across key stages 1–3. Similarly, effective teachers often take an apparently simple word such as 'change' and explore its varied use in disciplines such as science, PE, RE and history. History shares many words and concepts with other subjects: effective teaching about the use of language helps pupils understand how meanings behind them are common or different.

6 *Do our English or SEN co-ordinators offer advice about readability when history materials are purchased or home produced?*

Reading obstacles can be found in historical websites, television programmes, text and reference books. Their language can be made so linguistically simple that historical understanding is actually harder to get at. Or, they can become very complex as the writer pursues a balanced narrative. History co-ordinators can use readability tests to monitor such levels of difficulty in classroom materials. Effective schools co-ordinate the work of special needs and subject departments to support such awareness.

7 *How is our school's policy on English and literacy evident in history lessons, and how is the study of history pursued in literacy and English lessons?*

Pupils' ability to recognise words and letters, to listen, to take notes, to read text books as well as fiction, to discuss ideas, to work in groups, to know how to ask for help, to look words up in dictionaries or glossaries, to ask questions, to construct sentences, to critically and analytically watch television, to understand maps and diagrams, to interpret pictures, to use ICT, to write non-fiction with increasing length and depth: all are required in many history lessons and support the 'use of language across the curriculum'. None can be taught in history lessons alone. A whole school, inter-disciplinary and planned approach to literacy skills is essential from Key Stage 1 to Key Stage 3; something the English 'national literacy strategy' acknowledges but does not automatically facilitate in the context of a broad and balanced curriculum.

8 *How is history in our school made accessible and useful to children not yet literate in English?*

Pupils motivation to learn is essential in a discipline such as history. When taught well, history stimulates high quality thinking and discussion in children who may be learning English for the first time or who are struggling with literacy. At this point, insensitive or inappropriate feedback about 'correct spelling and punctuation' (DfEE 1999c p.40) can damage or destroy budding historical and linguistic development. Equally, the rich linguistic environment history provides can be used to reinforce and extend confidence about basic vocabulary, language protocols and rules of communication.

9 *How does our school promote critical literacy across different media?*

History is an interpretative discipline, often consisting of spoken, heard, written or read words but these are not the only aspects of the media upon which it draws to make its interpretations. Most pupils experience fine and commercial arts, 2D and 3D visual arts, architecture, music, landscape, TV and film, ICT, technology, food and drama in their history education, often regularly. Such fields have their own conventions and languages (semiotic codes). Teaching about them can be used to support pupils' ability to communicate effectively in written English as well as to enrich their history.

10 *How does our history and English curriculum challenge pupils to express and debate values by speaking, listening, reading and writing with increasing precision?*

The English national curriculum is more than mere subjects. It 'should aim to promote pupils' spiritual, moral, social and cultural development' (DfEE 1999c p. 11), as well helping students become thinking and participative 'informed citizens' (ibid. p. 184). The sort of language teachers use with and expect of pupils in history depends on such moral and educational, as well as purely historical values. For instance, teachers need to show that terms such as 'invasion' and 'exploration' have both been used to describe the same phenomenon, such as European incursions overseas post-Columbus. Effective communication by pupils needs teachers to provide motivating reasons and contexts in which to make meanings happen. History and its potential to spark debates about values can supply many of these.

11 *What specific steps, such as training events, meetings or team-teaching, has our school taken to co-ordinate the work of teachers of English and history?*

Developing students' powers of expression relies as much upon teaching them that historical words have different meanings and possible alter-natives, as it does upon decoding individual words. Teaching children to spell 'the glorious revolution' is not history. Teaching them to understand what revolution is, what that revolution was and why some Scots may not call it glorious, is history. Neither approach reaches full effectiveness without the other.

12 *In practice and through a child's eyes, just how inter-disciplinary is the curriculum in our school? Do we teach children about overlaps between 'ways of knowing' (e.g. stories in history and art, experiments in science and tech-nology) in the different subjects of the school curriculum?*

Eminent psychologists view knowledge rather differently to the models implied in the English national curriculum. Bruner for instance (1986) identified the 'narrative and paradigmatic' as fundamental modes of thought evident in cultures and individuals. He argued this was more basic to intellectual development than particular subjects or disciplines. Gardner (1993) identified seven different types of intelligence and argued that conventional modern schools barely developed most of them. If such ideas had any truth, the whole school curriculum might benefit from being much more inter-disciplinary. Within such an approach more common 'Use of language across the curriculum' would be acquire even more importance than at present.

II. Using Documents

'Using documents' reflects practice with teachers and archivists, examining how to improve students' use of language and historical thinking. It offers guidance without claiming to be definitive and touches upon the following underlying questions:

- *Does history learning increase or decrease a child's dependence on the teacher?*
- *To what extent does history teaching promote transmission or analysis of historical knowledge?*
- *Is history learning designed for groups or individuals?*
- *Are history curricula inter-disciplinary or subject specific?*

For school purposes 'historical documents' can be thought of as:

- *names (e.g. of people, places, buildings);*
- *memorials (e.g. gravestones, carved inscriptions, war memorials);*
- *manuscript sources (e.g. log books, letters, census returns, accounts);*
- *printed sources (e.g. directories, newspapers, books, reports);*
- *cartographic sources (e.g. OS or estate maps);*
- *oral sources (e.g. interviews, tapes, transcripts).*

Starting principles

- Start with a document describing people or actions. Try to use local examples to increase motivation and support a document with other sources such as photographs or oral history.
- Even if the document needs simplifying, always have the original or something close available to ALL children. Even if they cannot read the whole, most enjoy puzzling and cracking its 'code'.
- Read the document a few times yourself to grasp the main points and words, and decide on likely problems.
- Entitle the document and give information about author and provenance.
- When simplifying, do not be afraid to change the word or sentence order.
- It may be appropriate to alter the style (e.g. written to verbal).
- Decide how severe a simplification is needed: three levels is the most common.
- Reduce the document to individual sentences, phrases or words.
- Speak it before you read it, as you read it, and perhaps after reading it by having it on tape.
- Glossaries or visual clues may be useful.
- Consider accompanying evidence and teaching techniques to make it more accessible.
- Make simplifications with colleagues as a staff or year group: a valuable professional development activity with a practical outcome.
- Make it clear to students that YOU edited this, and that they can too.
- Tell students about the time, place and author from which the document comes – OR ask them to speculate on these.
- Introduce the idea that all documents are written for different reasons: can we see what they are for this one?

- Also ask: why has it come down to us now, how may it have been altered from its original condition and context, why are we choosing to spend time looking at it?
- Read the document out loud before distributing it. Often this can be done effectively as a story. Have taped versions available.
- Make history learning activities individually meaningful but linked to other curriculum areas such as English, ICT or Geography.

Some groundwork

1   Let children see documents through a visit to a record office or library, who can display a range of documents and explain how and why they preserve them.
2   Be enthusiastic about records. A reproduction of a Victorian directory is commonplace but its information is still original to the learner and highly motivating. Local records are often the most exciting since they stimulate a personal investment and curiosity.
3   Emphasise the scarcity value of historical data: once gone it is irreplaceable. Analogise with 'endangered species' or discuss whether children have ever lost anything precious. What happens to an old person's stories? What recent media examples of historical or archaeological 'finds' excite children's interest?
4   Collect and discuss 'documents' from home or school. Examples include class registers, school log books and records, shopping lists, birth and death certificates, passports, driving licences, bills, insurance certificates, etc.
5   Discuss the physical characteristics of particular documents, for example whether they are on parchment, vellum, paper, microfilm or fiche, photo-graphic paper and bound or loose leaf. How are these materials made or preserved?
6   Discuss the structure and purpose of a document: is it a bureaucratic form, a legal letter, a list, a diary, a description? Relate to contemporary examples and children's writing in similar genres.
7   Let children puzzle in pairs or groups over a hard document without any help. Encourage speculation for twenty minutes before children's guesses are compared to the modern English version. Then discuss the document's language, headings, appearance, possible purpose and age, words that we recognise and those we do not. If appropriate, introduce a simplified version of a document alongside the 'original'. Related simplification techniques include lists, abbreviations, condensing, precis, glossaries, key words, verbalisations, tapes, transcriptions, pictures and sketches.
8   An efficient use of ICT is to present versions of documents through word processing, database, spreadsheet, concept keyboard or scanning packages. The analytic capabilities of information-handling packages can then help students think about the document.
9   Start with documents that describe people or actions and use as many local examples as possible.

Some classroom activities

Introducing a wide range of documents stimulates more sophisticated reading, writing, talking, questioning and thinking. Most of the activities below focus upon aspects 3, 4 and 5 of national curriculum history's 'knowledge, skills and understanding' relating to historical interpretation, enquiry and organisation and communication. Depending upon the document chosen many also reinforce 'knowledge and understanding' of aspect 2 concerning the 'events, people and changes in the past' and can be linked to NC English (DfEE 1999a). They are presented in an approximate hierarchy of difficulty.

1 Draw three pictures to show the most important aspects of this document. Children use research from other sources such as books or TV, to make these pictures as authentic as possible to the period. Have other children drawn the same conclusions and pictures?

2 Draw a picture to put alongside the document in a book for children. Or research other books to find an appropriate historical picture. Explain why this one has been drawn or chosen.

3 Delete words from the copy of a document then ask children: what might go in there? Can we still work out the document's meaning? How do our guesses compare with the original? From a fraction of the document, can children guess what the whole document might say or be for?

4 Summarise what happens in a document into a number of key words. Or, find key words to show categories such as 'person – feeling – action – place, etc.' Compare and discuss different summaries.

5 Imagine you could question people who made the document or are mentioned in it. What would you ask? Use the document as a check list or prompt in an imagined interview with them.

6 Divide a document into sections, sentences or paragraphs for pairs or groups of children to decipher and summarise. Using group or whole class discussion, join the extracts to make the document 'complete' again.

7 As above but all children have all sections. Can they put them back into the original order? With a map or visual image, try a jigsaw.

8 Read a document carefully. If it was a newspaper story, what headline would you give it? For sophisticated learners, what about headlines for different newspapers representing opposing points of view?

9 Count some important nouns, adjectives, terms or images in the document. What does their frequency and nature tell us about the time the document came from?

10 Provide a 'faulty' summary of a document for children to check against the original and find the teacher' s deliberate mistakes. These can include obvious anachronisms. Let students know how many there are to start with!

11 Turn the document itself into an authentic-sounding story of the period, or make up a story that includes the document in it. If you can find different documents about the same person or event, supply them in a 'pack' to help students stage an historical reconstruction e.g. 'This is your life' or 'historical drama'.

12 Put the document into a classroom museum. What would the caption say about why this is an important document? How does it link to other pieces of evidence? Can they verbally explain their museum to a visitor?

13 Turn the document into a 'news report' of events at the time, drawing upon other research. Make it in contemporary TV, radio or newspaper style. Present a whole programme with different pieces of evidence linked together.

14 In a small group of 3 or 4, turn the document into a 'frozen picture' which explains what is happening and what is significant. As an extension task, allow the audience to ask questions of the people in the picture once they have seen the original document.

15 Ask one child to narrate the document out loud, whilst others mime what is happening and most significant in the document.

16 As a visual equivalent to (15), ask children to commentate upon archival images such as photographs or film. Demand of more advanced thinkers that they explain as well as describe what is seen.

17 After initial work on a document, ask students to answer different sorts of questions such as: the effects it may have had on different sorts of people who read it, what preceded and succeeded it for the people concerned. Stick a copy of the original onto large paper, with questions and answers arranged around. Students can link answers to make a more extended piece of writing.

18 Give children different documents on which they become 'experts' and are 'hot seated'. They explain a document and what it means to the history they are learning.

19 Ask children to order a group of documents by historical criteria: most or least trustworthy, how useful for giving information, how useful for asking questions, how relevant for this particular enquiry, for discovering about people such as young children, married women, rich people or agricultural workers?

20 Children imagine they are the person who first made this document. They describe the different things they would have done to make it using talk or writing a list or prose description.

21 Pretend this is the only document telling us about a particular thing. Deduce all that we can. Then introduce another source that supplements or contradicts the first. What do we think now and how has it changed?

22 Who or what sort of person might have gained and lost from this document being made or publicised? Make lists of the people mentioned in the document and ask the students to re-arrange them from most to least powerful, richest to poorest, etc.

23 Ask students to 'forge' a document having looked at some originals. Make it as convincing as they can in language, meaning, style, presentation. Then present it to a different audience: can they distinguish the fake from the original?

24 Imagine the 'talk' that might have happened whilst a document was being made. What would it have been about and can we re-enact it?

III. Improving Access to History? An ABC of Practice

This aspect of history teaching has been developed over the last decade with teachers of history and co-ordinators for special educational needs. The purpose is to help us communicate more effectively through text and talk with learners of history, whatever their level of linguistic attainment.

The following underlying questions are highlighted:

- *Does history teaching interact with the whole child or merely the student?*
- *Do communities promote singular or multicultural histories in schools?*
- *Are communities comprehensive or selective in their aspirations for history?*
- *Does history teaching standardise or differentiate pedagogy and materials?*

One key to making history accessible for all learners is to use a variety of historical sources: pictures, objects, music, film or site visits for instance, as well as computers, books and documents. Another is to use questions and materials which catch learners' interests but do not cover too much ground too quickly. A third is to have plenty of purposeful and varied talk in the history classroom, by teachers and children.

Written sources are still important to history and learners struggling with literacy need access to them. The following ideas ease that access:

Reconsider some 'simple' historical words

Think about how these historical words might be understood or misunderstood by young children struggling with English as a first or second language. We need to clarify such apparently simple, but actually ambiguous terms in history and English teaching. It is also useful to anticipate our own problematic examples:

Ancient	Growth	Popular
Britain	Idea	Power
Castle	King	Queen
Change	Land	Record
Class	Money	Ruler
Country	Old	Story
Estate	Order	Time
Fight	Past	War
Group	People	Wealth

Improving the accessibility of written curriculum materials

Are your school's home-produced or bought-in curriculum materials accessible to the children using them? The following points and processes will help you to improve the readability of historical materials:

1 Be aware of the terse, dense style of many text or information books and websites.
2 Use 'readability tests' but also rely on your professional intuition to decide whether a book will 'work' with your children.
3 Use key words and key ideas to explain a text via a blackboard, flipchart or OHT.
4 Ask children to use key words back to you.
5 Link texts to visual sources.
6 Sometimes teach directly from written texts, either with the teacher reading out loud or through group reading.
7 Ask children to underline words, sentences or passages which are:
   • incomprehensible
   • significant or interesting
   • showing something that is only 'maybe' (interpretations)
   • showing something they have come across before (where?)
8 Copy and cut passages up then ask children to reorder them: often there is more than one solution.
9 Delete headings and sub-headings then ask children to put their own in.
10 Rewrite or re-talk factual text in other forms such as dialogue, interview, letter or poem.
11 Give children sustained time to read demanding historical texts and plan for them to do so.
12 Teach children how to break down long sentences and how to scan and skim texts.
13 Let children question you on a text: 'test the teacher'.
14 Arrange for children to read texts in groups and set questions for other groups.
15 Structure reporting tasks so that as teacher you can assess and intervene where necessary.
16 Simplify and prepare your own 'original' historical materials.
17 Back up non-fiction texts with fiction and vice versa.
18 Dilute written text with double spacing, large print, broken up sections, diagrams and illustrations.
19 Allow people in text or talk to make actions and so illustrate ideas in a concrete way.
20 Use dialogue in text or talk to slow things down.
21 Add human details and explorations of motivations to improve accessibility.
22 Ask children to interact with the text in as many ways as possible.
23 Use momentum in written materials: repeat related ideas and words to build understanding.
24 Use narrative methods in writing and talking. Analysis of younger readers' use of texts shows fiction as more accessible than conventional non-fiction because:
   • it has more direct speech;
   • it tends to be person-centred and have people as agents of action;
   • it is closer to everyday language;

- it has more pronouns, mostly personal;
- narrative texts tend to be chronologic and cumulative;
- storied structures are familiar to children;
- fiction connects subject and verb more closely;
- fiction has more verbs and is less passive than non-fiction;
- non-fiction noun-phrases tend to be longer and more complex.

Improving the accessibility of teacher-talk

1 When speaking to the whole class keep exposition short. Check whether you are carrying all children with you by monitoring individuals of differing attainment.
2 Read non-fiction extracts out loud and translate what these 'mean' into your own words.
3 Use simple vocabulary and syntax to frame especially important and complex words.
4 Use child-speak and slang when appropriate and comfortable.
5 Avoid abstractions. Prepare a plan for a lesson then, following the advice of the late John Fines, take five steps back to understand children's starting points.
6 Use analogies sparingly and only if familiar to children.
7 Do not skate over a difficult historical topic such as 'industry' or 'evidence'. Neat summaries can so over-simplify an idea that children cannot gain a foothold. Clear explanations need details for children's thinking to hang on to.
8 Structure and define tasks clearly. For instance 'writing an explanation' is too general. Clarifying who, what, how and why things link together to make an explanation makes explanatory thinking easier to achieve.
9 Discuss, define, record and revisit unfamiliar words as regularly as possible.
10 Remain wary of history's many linguistic traps.

IV. Building Curriculum

The national curriculum offers a structure for a school's history curriculum, but its mandatory requirements can be met in different ways. This paper is a stimulus to rethinking structure in your history curriculum. It is especially useful in considering the following of this book's underlying questions:

- *Does the history curriculum open adults' values to scrutiny or promote their acceptance? Reveal or obscure the grounds for history's claims to value?*
- *Is the history curriculum inter-disciplinary or subject specific?*
- *Is the history curriculum locally or nationally defined?*

A methodology

For this book's writer, school history is *'the construction and deconstruction of explanatory narratives about the past, derived from evidence and in answer to questions'*. This can be explained to children as 'using questions and evidence to take apart and put together again real stories about the past' (see also Bage 1999a).

Maybe you can devise a better definition for your particular needs, using building blocks from this book and your own experience. Wherever your inspiration comes from you need to write this into a subject policy statement to explain history to colleagues, parents, governors, inspectors and children.

Build into your plans explanations of why we teach children history. As a test, think about this. Could your children say something convincing to you or their family about *what* they are doing when they study history, and *why*? If not, then perhaps your school's definition of history is not yet clear enough.

Some methods

Thinking history means asking questions of evidence. Here are some useful prompts for history questions and assessment:

> *Who, how, what, where, why, when, in what order, which, if, whether, did, can, try, find, search, could, might, research, enquire, should, choose, because, since, compare, think, remember, tell, explain, show, list, order, imagine, what if, what else?*

Apply them to the following sources of evidence, spread across the periods studied, and you will more than fulfil national curriculum history requirements:

Pictures	Words	Buildings
Videos	Books	Maps
People	Stories	Landscapes
Sites	Documents	Archaeology
Artefacts	Music	Museums
ICT	The media	Ourselves

Some content

The national curriculum tends to organise history chronologically by dividing it into periods and epochs. There are other ways to think about the curriculum, either to overlay or supplement such chronologies. For instance children might study history to help them think about the following themes in their local, national, continental and global pasts:

Homes	Gender	Science	Wars
Families	Health	Art	Rulers
Communities	Buildings	Words	Ruled
Clothes	Jobs	Music	Power
Food	Technology	Laws	Money
Tools	Leisure	Beliefs	Countries

Some ideas

The following concepts and terms are fundamental to thinking about history.

Chronology	Reason	Ideas	Questions	Stories
Sequence/order	Change	Descriptions	Answers	Arguments
Expressions of	Result	Viewpoints	Evidence	Explanations
time	Difference	Interpretations	Information	Descriptions
Then/now	Comparison	Attitudes	Selection	Presentations
Dates	Similarity	Values	Enquiries	Debates
Events	Continuity		Accuracy	Illustrations
Periods	Significance			Re-enactments
	Links			
	Trends			

- *Should all lessons contain something from each section if they claim to be history? Or, if we are teaching some history methodology, method, content and ideas, could we be confident that we were covering the 'national' curriculum?*

8 History and Communities in Practice

A. Why History is Useful in Schools

This paper was first written by the author in 1998 as an open letter on behalf of the Historical Association to the then Secretary of State for Education, David Blunkett. It argued for the continued inclusion of history in the primary national curriculum, at a point when the programmes of study for history and the other 'foundation subjects' had been suspended. It has been edited and amended slightly for inclusion in this book, since its arguments extend across the age range 4 to 14.

The document helps us consider the following underlying questions in this book:

- *Is history learning pursued for intrinsic or extrinsic ends?*
- *Do history curricula reveal or obscure the grounds for history's claims to value?*
- *To what extent do history curricula open adults' values to scrutiny or promote their acceptance?*
- *Should history curricula be locally or nationally defined?*
- *Do communities understand history as school work or lifelong knowledge?*

The Context

We are writing to express grave concerns about two events. One is the imminent suspension of the programme of study for history in the National Curriculum: the second is the forthcoming national curriculum review. We also wish to offer constructive suggestions for how history in schools can support education policy within a slimmer statutory curriculum.

1 In the government's own words 'A good education provides access to this country's rich and diverse culture, to its history and to an understanding of its place in the world ... to the best that has been thought and said and done' (DfEE 1997 p.9). Learning history is central to such a vision. It supports many of the government's aims and priorities for schooling and makes unique contributions to children's literacy, citizenship and personal and moral education.

2 Narrow interpretations of literacy and numeracy initiatives can undermine government aims articulated above and dominate school curricula, as schools and teachers struggle to achieve large improvements in measurable

standards via SATs or public exams. Government policies and supporting documentation generally neither refer to this dilemma nor explore its resolution.

3 Primary history in the national curriculum has resulted in significant and continuing educational advances according to the government's own inspection data (e.g. Hamer 1997; Woodhead 1997 p.13).

4 Like business, teachers need clear frameworks within which to plan effectively. Curriculum policy should support this through considered thinking over twelve year timespans, a child's minimum timespan in school, as well as by focusing minds on measurable shorter-term targets. We trust that educational planning will continue to balance such needs and widely communicate, for instance, findings that 'schools which did well in [the 1996 KS2 SATS] also provided a broad and balanced curriculum' (OFSTED 1997 p. 1).

History's contribution to four fundamentals

The aims and purposes of the whole curriculum

The Historical Association agrees with the two over-arching aims for the school curriculum discussed in national documentation (e.g. DfEE 1999b pp. 10–13) and anticipates continuing to help develop a history curriculum that can provide what taxpayers expect from the educational system. We also observe that learning history develops thinking skills which will remain fundamental to the people, economies and societies of the twenty-first century:

- Tackling problems – e.g. *how many different ways are there to research life in our school or village fifty years ago?*
- Analysing and interpreting historical evidence – e.g. *after our museum visit what can we say about the ancient Egyptians?*
- Organising information through arguments – e.g. *how can we decide whether the Romans made things better or worse for the Celts, or the industrial revolution improved the status of women?*
- Communicating effectively – e.g. *how can you tell us what you learned from interviewing your grandparents?*
- Understanding change and continuity – e.g. *how has our town changed since 1800?*
- Learning through and about other people's experiences – e.g. *what do people in your family remember about their childhood?*
- Asking and prompting real and interesting questions – e.g. *what was this object used for, and why was it so important in the past?*
- Knowing more about their local, national, European and world identities – e.g. *what does history tell us about the meaning of being English?*
- Seeing where human values, ideas and organisations have come from – e.g. *how and why were people punished for what they believed in Tudor times?*
- Encouraging curiosity and constructive scepticism – e.g. *how accurate and trustworthy are these wartime films and posters?*

Raising standards within the national curriculum

Recent and extensive professional experience, research and inspection (e.g. Bage, Lister and Grisdale 1999; Counsell 1997; Cooper 1995a and b; Fines and Nichol 1997; Hamer 1997; Hoodless 1998; Wray and Lewis 1997) demonstrate how *history develops children's literacy by*:

- Introducing and consolidating writing, reading and speaking skills;
- Enticing children to read and construct stories of the past;
- Teaching how different media communicate information and ideas;
- Expanding vocabulary through rich descriptions of people, places and events;
- Teaching children the stories behind everyday words;
- Motivating children to learn basic and advanced study skills.

History is vital to literacy and young children are highly motivated by reading history in school and beyond. History also contributes to a *broad and balanced curriculum by*:

- Developing individual and collective senses of identity;
- Exploring the diverse heritage of different cultures and nations;
- Giving children firsthand experiences of fieldwork in rural and urban environments;
- Providing an ideal basis for cross-curricular and project work;
- Developing children's knowledge and understanding of other peoples and cultures;
- Offering real, varied contexts for children to practise ICT, numeracy and social skills.

Unless taught how to view history critically children are prey to political and commercial propaganda about the past. Curiosity, imagination and healthy scepticism are nurtured by history's numerous and interesting stories. History develops *citizenship* and puts 'the real needs of children at the curriculum's centre' (Morris, June 1997) by:

- Raising children's awareness of ethical and moral issues;
- Enabling children to read, view and listen critically;
- Opening stories of a child's locality, region, nation and world;
- Giving children a sense of the plurality and diversity of people's lives;
- Encouraging children to develop opinions based upon their reason and interpretations of evidence;
- Showing children how democracy has evolved and continues to be developed.

Children's senses of moral awareness, common citizenship and personal identity are fostered by history. History plays a central role in introducing children to society's values and in helping individual children to improve their own educational achievement.

Lifelong learning and the World of Work

History has never been a more popular family pursuit, leisure activity or subject for study in adult or higher education (e.g. Anderson 1997; Lowenthal 1998; Samuel 1994). People profit from learning history throughout their lives because it:

- Develops skills, qualities and ideas, especially literacy and information handling, to support independent and lifelong learning;
- Is familiar to parents from their education, so families can help their children with it;
- Offers roots and identities, especially through family or local history, which are increasingly important for social cohesion at a time of rapid and millennial change;
- Supports the heritage and tourism industries and is essential to the survival and expansion of museums and the historic environment;
- Encourages clearer and more active citizenship.

The age of eleven is too late to start the study of history because:

- Children experience interpretations of history, culture and heritage through television and other mass media from pre-school ages. Who will teach them how to make sense of these if schools do not, through history?
- Learning history in the primary age ranges helps found numerous desirable and marketable key skills such as communication, working with others, improving children's own learning, problem-solving and thinking skills, increasing confidence with ICT;
- England, different localities and the world simply contains too much history for it only to be learned about in the three years between the ages of 11 and 14.

Teacher creativity and curriculum flexibility

As an education minister emphasised (Morris, June 1997) teachers need exciting, child-friendly content with which to interest children in literacy, numeracy and ICT within schools; and in libraries, information sources and the many worlds of thinking and culture beyond schools. History offers these in abundance and it would be wasteful to ignore its resources. A flexible but minimal core of statutory history curriculum content and skills helps promote high academic expectations in the following ways:

- History's content (e.g. 'The Aztecs') and intellectual demands (e.g. 'knowledge, skills and understanding') are highly inter-disciplinary, offering numerous focal points for projects extending into literacy, ICT and numeracy, as well as across the curriculum;

- There is a settled consensus that the thinking skills described by the various national curricula are central to history and have improved standards;
- Materials for local history and local examples of national history were developed extensively in schools during the 1990s, curriculum investment which can continue to yield valuable educational returns;
- Teacher-designed or more flexible studies of history can be accommodated within a national history curriculum framework.

We would argue for as much local discretion over content as possible, with national statutory requirements remaining for core content, skills, concepts and issues of equity.

B. Local History: Best Practice?

These ideas were developed during collaborations for local history projects with teachers, archivists and museum education officers and summarise ten principles to underpin any local history project. They are especially useful in considering the following underlying questions about whether:

- *Communities are active or passive in pursuit of their own histories?*
- *Understand history as school work or lifelong knowledge?*
- *View schools or central government as key controllers of the curriculum?*
- *History teaching interacts with the whole child or only the student?*

1. **Local history is resource-led.** Find out the broad scope of the records available in a given field of enquiry such as Victorian education, or local experiences of World War II. Only then decide whether or how to focus upon it. This means broad teacher planning a term in advance, to finalise whether topics have sufficient or inappropriate evidence to support an educational enquiry.
2. Within this broad teacher-led framework **local history should be child-centred.** In some projects, the teacher seems to be doing more work than the children. The best examples balance both, with teacher pre-planning supporting students' spontaneity and genuine enquiries.
3. **Local history should be enquiry-led.** There is no better place for children to 'act as historians' than when researching an area with which they are familiar, or which is accessible for visits.
4. **Record the enquiry and its research questions.** Celebrate curiosity and analysis by using children's questions to scaffold a project. Record them as the spine of displays, have a 'questions corner', ask children to write them down in lists or flowcharts.
5. **Use the widest range of historical sources possible.** Most local history studies can incorporate museum and site visits, oral history, artefacts, maps, photographs, pictures, publications, printed and handwritten documents.

Highlight different sources by naming and discussing them with students: this makes their learning about such sources transferrable to their next history study.

6 **Find romance.** An interesting 'way in' to local history is the allure of 'what has been lost?' Look for small clues from which pupils can build a wider picture: faded lettering on a wall, a bump in a field, an entry in a school log-book, a name on a map. These can lead us into wanting to know more: most children love a mystery.

7 **Evaluate evidence.** When drawing conclusions, stick to ideas for which we have evidence. Most localities have apophrycal tales of why this factory is there, or this house is called that. Collect these, but can your project also test them out? Build understanding of the concepts of evidence and deduction through an interesting local mystery.

8 **Involve local experts** as inspiration for children, teachers, classroom assistants and volunteers. Local authors, amateur archeologists, archivists, antique dealers, responsible metal detector enthusiasts, vicars, builders or architects, radio or newspaper journalists: such people possess stories and expertise to enthuse children. Preparation and discrimination is needed because local enthusiasts can be boring; but somebody who loves their subject, likes children and talks clearly rarely goes wrong.

9 **Involve the local community.** Often this is as a source of information: record offices, libraries, websites, buildings, parish magazines or newsletters, letters home, contacts with ex-teachers or pupils, local history groups, local newspapers and supplements, the church, old people's homes etc. can be exciting sources of evidence. Local people can also act as consultants, classroom helpers and audience (see Figure 8.1).

10 **Aim for an end-product.** An exhibition, open evening, drama production, publication, school museum, radio programme, folder, group presentation in assembly: there are many ways of communicating the results of historical enquiry. This not only gives the local community something back and boosts the image of the school: it is also educationally apt. Part of 'being an historian' is communicating the results of historical enquiry in clear and suitable ways.

C. Lessons from Foxfire

Figure 8.1 Ten Foxfire Practices (adapted from Wigginton 1989)

> *The FOXFIRE project was discussed in Chapter 4. As the following practices reveal, at its heart lies the belief that education should reflect and connect with the communities beyond school which the education system claims to serve. The exploration of local culture and history is therefore a key component in a Foxfire curriculum. This book has argued that similar things have already been achieved in England and can be extended further. The hope is that teachers can critically mediate national educational structures into local and community-led learning. This paper illustrates such a vision in the context of the English 1999 national curriculum in history, taking examples from the following mandatory studies:*

- *KS1 The way of life of people in the more distant past who lived in the local area or elsewhere in Britain.*
- *KS2 Britain and the wider world in Tudor times*
- *KS3 A world study after 1900*

The document helps consider questions underlying this book such as:

- *Do communities view schools or central government as key controllers of the curriculum?*
- *Do communities promote singular or multicultural histories in schools?*
- *Are communities active or passive in pursuit of their own histories?*
- *Do communities perceive historical knowledge as made individually or collectively?*

1   'All the work teachers and students do together must flow from student desire . . . infused from the beginning with student choice, design, revision, execution, reflection, and evaluation' (Wigginton 1989 pp. 26–8).

- KS1   Which people from the past would we most like to find out about?
- KS2   What do we want to find out about 'Tudor times' – and what do we want to learn whilst we are doing that?
- KS3   What might learning about the history of the world after 1900 teach us?

2   'Connections of the work to the surrounding community and the real world outside the classroom are clear' (ibid.).

- KS1   Which people and what things in our community can help us find out about people who are now dead and so cannot tell us for themselves?
- KS2   What people, buildings or things from our community can help us find out about people and things from 500 years ago? Who can teach us how to learn from these things?
- KS3   Who can we speak to in our community who has taken part in world history since 1900?

3   'The work is characterised by student action rather than the passive receipt of processed information . . . students . . . must be led continually into new work and unfamiliar territory' (ibid.).

- KS1   What tools can we use to step inside the minds of people from a long time ago?
- KS2   How can I become expert in something from the sixteenth century?
- KS3   What can we learn from and about twentieth century 'technologies' such as the Internet, television, film and radio?

4   'A constant feature of the process is its emphasis on peer teaching, small-group work, and teamwork' (ibid.).

- KS1   If there are people in our school who have learnt about this before, what can they tell us?
- KS2   How can we divide ourselves into groups who can become experts on particular people or places from Tudor times?
- KS3   How can our class or year group organise itself to bring together the results of our individual enquiries and interviews?

5   'The role of the teacher is that of collaborator and team leader and guide, rather than boss or the repositry of all knowledge' (ibid.).

- KS1   How can I build upon my children's expanding language and thinking skills through this study?
- KS2   As a teacher and an adult, what don't I know about the sixteenth century?
- KS3   How might I use my personal or family history to illustrate for my students some of the problems and themes that this study could throw up?

6   'There must be an audience beyond the teacher for student work . . . another individual, or a small group, or the community' (ibid).

- KS1   How shall we tell our families what we have been learning about in history this term?
- KS2   How can we turn our classroom into a 'sixteenth century experience' for other classes to visit?
- KS3   Who outside of school will be interested to hear our community's links to twentieth century history, and how shall we tell them?

7   'The academic integrity of the work must be absolutely clear. Rather than subverting, avoiding, or skirting around any state-mandated skills and content list . . . accept that agenda, accomplish it, but also go far beyond its normally narrow confines' (ibid.).

- KS1   How could our history enquiry be a stimulus to create and perform art, music and dance?
- KS2   Where did the monarchy in England come from and do we still need them?
- KS3   Does what we have learnt about twentieth century history teach us anything about the problems that twenty-first century adolescents encounter such as: racism, unemployment, sexism, poor housing or drug abuse?

8   'The work must include unstintingly honest, ongoing evaluation for skills and/or content, and changes in student attitudes . . . In the service of these goals, teachers and students must become researchers together, examining not only teaching methods but learning itself' (ibid.).

- KS1   How can we record what we did learn from this project, and what we did not learn but wished we had?
- KS2   What do the people who visited our sixteenth century classroom experience really think about what they saw?
- KS3   As a student, what did speaking to older people teach me about learning history and about growing old?

9   'As the year progresses, new activities should grow gracefully out of the old' (ibid.).

- KS1   What famous people or events were touched on in our enquiry and which would we like to find out more about?
- KS2   What questions does our study leave us with about subjects such as religion, poverty or museums?

- KS3 How do the experiences of the people we have spoken to compare with what writers, scientists or artists tell us about twentieth century world history?

10 'As students become more thoughtful participants in their own education, our goals must be to help them become increasingly able and willing to guide their own learning, fearlessly, for the rest of their lives.' (ibid.)

- KS1 What did I do best in this project that I would like to do more of?
- KS2 If I had to write five things to do (or avoid) for somebody learning the same thing next year, what would they be?
- KS3 What did the people to whom I spoke or presented work tell me about how to learn from life; how much do I agree or disagree with what they said?

D. The Seven Ages of Sancho

In its present form this story derives from the TASTE (teaching-as-storytelling) project in Greenwich, London. Some of this project's work has been described elsewhere (e.g. Bage 2000a, 2000b; Collins 1999, 2000a). This particular story is included as an example of how national and international history can be made local and inter-disciplinary, reflecting the communities which history and education serve. It was devised from a model pack of materials (Dingsdale 1998) which reproduces 18th century engravings, portraits, plans, letters, musical scores and much else for educational use. Teachers' notes explain how the life of Ignatius Sancho (1729–80), a black and orphaned slave child who spent much of his life in Greenwich, can support the teaching and learning of history, art, English and other subjects across the 4–14 age range

> *Writer, musician, composer, entrepreneur, critic, valet and butler, friend to duchesses, dukes, slaves and artists, Ignatius Sancho was all of these. But he was also orphaned at birth, brought up as a slave in a household where servants should not learn to read . . . He educated himself in the face of discouragement . . . He learned to play and write music . . . He wrote plays and attempted acting . . . But above all he made friends. They included dukes, duchesses, artists and paupers who needed clothes for warmth . . . He saw himself as both an African and an Englishman.*
>
> *(ibid. Section 1.0 Introduction)*

This version was told and written to offer the story to local schools and communities in succinct and accessible form. It is rooted in evidence, attempts to reflect Sancho's life and has been used with children, teachers and the local community.

The story helps us consider the following questions underlying this book:

- *Do communities promote singular or multicultural histories in schools?*

- *To what extent do communities interact with their history through popular as well as specialist media?*
- *Do history curricula open adults' values to scrutiny or promote their acceptance?*
- *Do communities perceive historical knowledge as made individually or collectively?*

· · · · ·

This story's first age starts with a baby. A creaking ship was his home, sails puffed with African air, holds crammed with African souls. The boat lolled and leaned on the salty swell, between the West coast of Africa, ensnared by slaving; and the coast of the Caribs to where the ship sailed. Here the baby was brought to birth, hope amongst the helpless. Here his mother was levelled by death, casual cruelty amongst the countless. Who would love that baby now?

Who? The bishop, of course. The bishop took the orphan and christened him. '*Ignatius*,' he crooned 'I christen you *Ignatius*. He was a saint of great learning.' Then shouting to the crowd pressed in at the auction: 'Where is a woman with milk, willing to suckle this scrap?'

The scrap suckled well on a slave-woman's milk. Quicker than you can say *Ignatius* the babe was a toddler, but this boy toddled further than most. Sailing east from the Spanish West Indies with a captain unknown, the ship beached safe on a stranger's coast. A grey river thronged with ships and sails. A smoked and teeming city, crowded with carriages and carts. A thriving, greedy country washed with money and merchants. A country called England, a city called London, a river called Thames and a village called Greenwich. Who would love this toddler now?

The sisters, of course. 'We will' they piped, 'we'll bid our money to love that black toddler. We will make him our servant in fine velvet cloth. He can polish glasses, fetch the sewing, pour tea into cups. He will welcome our guests with his bonny black face. Then just for his luck and for fine Christian love, we shall add one more name to *Ignatius*. *Sancho* we shall say, *Ignatius Sancho*: god bless our little black boy.'

So the second age began: a child petted and plumped by three maiden sisters, a toddling trinket of turbans and twirls. The tale of a toddler to a boy, growing with three sisters in Greenwich. Years passed, from small boy to big boy. Years passed, from kisses and curls to roughing and tumbling, learning and loving and books and belles. Before the boy knew it he towered over the sisters: the world loomed large and the sisters seemed small.

'He's chipped the blue china,' the eldest complained. 'He borrows my books,' the youngest whined. 'He . . . well I cannot full say,' the middle one blushed 'but Harriet the housemaid flushed as pink as a rose.'

So who will love this boy now, teenaged and clumsy, as in the third age he turns to a man?

'I will,' said the Duke 'I will have the boy and make him my man. He's a strapping handsome fellow, as fine as they come. He will work for me in my mansion at Blackheath. I will lend him my books, teach him my music, he can serve as my man in the Montagu house.'

Which Ignatius Sancho did, with great glee. How far had that friendless, slave-baby come? From orphan on the ocean to the grand Duke of Montagu. From gangs and plantations to Greenwich and London. From baby, to toddler, to teenager and now: a dashing and handsome man-about-town. A fine figure he cut in brass-buttoned blue jacket, black shining shoes and starched snow-white shirt.

Ignatius: so refined that he talked with the town. The Montagues paraded in carriages fine, the Montagues and *Ignatius* too. To theatres packed with powdered wigs and painted ladies, to concerts strung with violins and sopranos, to churches blessed with black robes and rectors. Ignatius drank it all in, then talked it all out.

And how could Ignatius read! Ignatius loved books from the first moment he saw one, so he taught himself to read and to write. And how could Ignatius write! Not just letters to famous people, not just poems, but songs and dances and tunes which were published. And how could Ignatius play and dance to his music! Servant, butler, gentleman's gentleman. Writer, musician, friend: in his fourth age this black man took London by storm. But would London love him, forever?

So a fifth age dawned, better than the last: an age of lasting love. Though girls had giggled, women had winked when warmed by Ignatius's smile, his life was too fizzing and full for love. Until Ann. Ignatius thought he had everything – until Ann. Ignatius thought he was happy – until Ann, gorgeous Ann. Ignatius served only his master – until Ann: Ann who was beautiful, Ann who was black, Ann who was London and English like him.

From babe to toddler, to teenager, to man: and now to lover and father. Ignatius married Ann Osborne and soon some little Sanchos started: 'Sanchonettas' he called them himself. There was Kitty, Betsy, Lydia, Mary, Fanny and last of all, William.

The fifth age flashed by as the little ones grew: but Ignatius was growing too. Not richer, for growing families gobble cash. Ignatius was growing rounder. Ignatius had always loved life, and food too. As the heart swells through love so the belly swells through food and Ignatius' belly swelled round. Finally too, he grew tired. He had loved riding with Duke Montagu in fine carriages, seeing the country and swanning round town! With children, life was different. The back was stiffer, the belly bulged bigger and the wallet wasted away. Time to settle down, time for a change. So who would love him now?

Everybody, that's who. So the sixth age began, a life nearly of ease. With the aid of his Duke, Ignatius opened a shop. With the help of his friends, he sold things. What should a shop in this great city London, what should a black shopkeeper sell? Ignatius wondered. He asked round his friends. He thought about his life of twists and turns: of his brothers, black brothers, and sisters in slavery. Could he sell in his shop what their labours produced: help himself and at the same time, help them?

So the sixth age passed: in guineas and gold for tea, silver and florins for sugar and often, in pennies and halfpennies for snuff. Ignatius became a grocer, small shop awash with the smells of trade and the goods of empire. Tobacco and its smoke, tea and its talk wafted from the door to tempt in the shopper. Ignatius never made his fortune and if he had, he would have spent it. For if truth be told Ignatius was an easy-going man. He took Ann and the girls to concerts, read people's books, wrote letters and songs to those in high places. Authors and artists dropped by with their friends, trade trickled in, months and years sped by.

What of Sancho's seventh age? Ignatius died in the year 1780. Who would love him now and who would love his family? A friend would. To remember Ignatius she made a book of his letters. It sold many copies and earned £500, given to help his children and wife. God would, for Ignatius was a Christian. We would too, storytellers and story listeners. For Ignatius lives today as one day we all will: lives as words in a story and as memory, in mind.

Section 3
Prospect

9 Thinking History Conclusions

> Once I had decided upon this second visit, I no longer thought of this
> pilgrimage into the past as a foolish and self-indulgent thing. It seemed, on
> the contrary, to be a journey of the utmost importance: until I had made it, I
> would not be able to begin upon the future set down in my palm or indeed
> upon any version of the future whatsoever.
>
> (Tremain 1989 p. 371)

Introduction

This book and our journey are now drawing towards . . . what? A destination
perhaps? This is true in the sense that we moved through a series of arguments
between Chapters 1 and 8, measuring our steps against a current educational
standard: that of the 2000 English national curriculum in history. Different
stages emphasised different dimensions. In Chapters 1 to 4 the emphasis was
upon retrospection and theory, introducing important ideas and lessons from
research and scholarship to throw light on current thinking. Chapters 5 to 8 led
with introspection and practice, offering a series of advisory, policy and
discussion documents focused on particular and perhaps more immediate needs.
This concluding chapter will tie a thread of the book by speculating briefly about
what may be some important prospective developments for future history
educators. A chronological progression sketching past, present and future has
therefore helped organise some of this book's thinking.

It is not the whole story, though. This chronology overlaid another linear
construct, tracing lines of educational latitude and longitude. Issues of governance, diversity, media, values, democracy, cognition and social context were
juxtaposed against the themes of learning, teaching, curriculum and community.
The purpose was to extrapolate some underlying questions embedded in the
practices of history education; and to clarify educational choices which thinking
people face, whatever the particular instance of 'curriculum' with which they are
grappling.

These dimensions may have been imaginary, in that I as writer invented their
form; but they aspired to reflect underlying, even predictable educational
regularities. In this sense this book's end destination has been expected all along.
What is less predictable are the senses you as reader have made of them. Your

journey through this book's ideas, as with your passage through history and education, is an individual route taken at a pace and directed towards ends of your own particular choosing. In other words this book, like all books, has had two 'destinations'. One has been the predictable, authorial ambition to progress from introduction through chapters to the present conclusion; the other an unpredictable, readerly journey concluding . . . where, and with what? During both I would hope that you have constantly evaluated the book's ideas against your own experience, values and desires. The foundation of the book upon a 'map of thinking history' was explicitly designed to assist this: so far as possible the desire was to liberate you, as reader, from the clutches of me, as writer, by revealing from the beginning some places which I hoped we would visit. Nevertheless the choice of whether you have gone to these places, and of whether you stay in them in future, remains entirely yours.

The concluding criterion against which I would like you to judge this book is not that as reader you have 'liked' or 'disliked' these places; but that visits to them have been of value and interest, if only to confirm the superiority of home. If you can carry a slighly more informed sense of individuality, of critical mediation, of confidence into your educational future then I will judge this book successful: but what might your future hold, on a broader level?

If history uses imagination to reconstruct the past, perhaps education uses imagination to construct the future. The concluding discussion synthesises these strands: less to predict the future, more to enrich the present by imagining what that future could hold. Such speculations will cluster around questions of the seven issues identified in our opening map: governance, diversity, media, values, democracy, cognition and society.

Who decides what?

Presaging the curriculum review of which the 2000 English history curriculum was a result, Alexander recently argued that 'There are two main lessons of history . . . The first is that we are unable to break free of it. The second, not entirely a paradox, is that people of power and influence tend to act as though history has nothing to teach them' (Alexander 1998 p. 61).

The first of these lessons has been borne out by the almost unchanged content and structure of the 'new' (2000) national curriculum in history, as compared to its predecessors. If the future is to be a radical improvement over the present the second lesson also needs heeding. The wider curriculum should not be a political plaything under the direct control of a small circle of ministers, civil servants and unelected advisers. Equally, in pre-national curriculum days it should never have been left entirely to individual teachers idiosyncratically to construct curricula for 'their' classrooms or schools. What might enrich our future is to develop a system of curriculum design synthesising the advantages of both extremes; history may be an excellent school subject through which to anticipate that improvement. A rich and political debate needs to be conducted about what sort of national identity a national history curriculum might enable for English peoples of the twenty-first century. Then, having led and properly influenced that debate, politicians should pledge to retreat from meddling with details, leaving the development and management of the curriculum to an independent and properly funded curriculum body representing education's different stakeholders. Meanwhile, that curriculum body should itself concentrate upon maximising curricular choice at local levels: not because this is an 'easy' option for teachers, governors or learners, but because it demands more of them. If a supposed 'lesson' of late twentieth century economic history was that central planning and control was counter-productive in financial or industrial markets, how can it possibly work in the freer and more open market of the mind: especially in cultures with ballooning access to multimedia and multi-channels? A fine-detailed, fussy and centralised national curriculum is a hopelessly anachronistic answer to the question 'who should decide what the history curriculum contains?' Families, teachers, communities and learners need to answer that question for themselves, within a minimal but democratically constructed framework. Curriculum development would become localised and concurrently, perhaps better reflect contemporary academic thinking about 'history's' future:

> . . . our public problems derive in the end from our personal selves, so that what is needed is a study of how we came to be the sorts of people that we are, of why we have the perceptions, the outlooks and the attitudes that we have. Such a study must clearly in large part be historical, but it needs to include practical as well as theoretical dimensions, sciences and social sciences as well as arts. It would constitute the ultimate humanistic discipline . . .
>
> (Southgate 1996 p. 137)

Such a path has been trodden before, notably in the 1960s and 1970s by the MACOS curriculum of 'Man A Course of Study' (e.g. Bruner 1983; Dow 1991); and in the 1970s and 1980s by the Humanites Curriculum Project (e.g. HCP 1970; Stenhouse 1975). If it was trodden again the hope would be to synthesise the pedagogic integrity of the HCP, the quality of materials of MACOS and the unifying hopes of post-1988 English national curricula, with a new ambition for the English history curriculum to be locally and regionally interpreted. This leads inexorably to the next question.

Diversifying Englishness?

Can we build a curriculum in England not just to include all English people, but to clarify what is historically distinctive, worst and best about being English? A brilliant recent study of bilingual language learning perhaps highlights parallel possibilities for a discipline such as history. It opens with a picture of the locality of a case-study school, itself worth quoting:

> Over the arched doorways two plaster figures, a boy and a girl in 18th century dress, look down over the children as they thread their way to school between the sober-suited ranks of city workers . . . The mothers gather around the gate, unaware that on this very spot in 1888 the Ripper's fifth

victim was found, and shepherd their children into class, where they settle on the rug: John whose parents are from Nigeria, Azad whose family is from Bangladesh; Wesley whose grandparents are in Jamaica; Sally whose parents have come down from Lancashire. Mrs. Kelly, born in London of Irish parents, welcomes her class . . . Since the Middle Ages, this area bordering the City of London has housed the newcomers . . .

(Williams 1997 pp. 89–90)

Close observations of children in this school revealed the 'crucial role played by family members other than parents in supporting the child's reading' (ibid. p. 94), citing in particular a grandfather's influence. Meanwhile in an adjaceant article in the same publication, Rashid and Gregory (1997) describe how 'structured story' can build the learning of English as an additional language from within multicultural strengths. Using traditional tales, well known in English and other cultures, this technique divided 'story reading into stages . . . easily recognisable by the child . . . grounded on the advanced metalinguistic awareness shown by many young bilinguals' (Williams 1997 p. 116).

History perhaps needs an equivalent national curriculum structure. This would not simply 'allow' learners and educators to build on the rich and diverse historical foundations of localities, families, oral histories or stories as described above, in the essentially one-off 'local studies' that dominate present pedagogic practice. Rather it would demand, as many fine teachers currently achieve, that any English national history curriculum should be filterered through local and regional sieves.

A more promising *locale* for exploring local, national and international history than the one described above is difficult to imagine, richer perhaps in curriculum or cultural terms than supposedly 'favoured' suburbs. The imposition of a one-fits-all 'national' British curriculum onto such a locality runs the danger not just of pandering to cultural or biological racism (Cole 1998; Short and Carrington 1998). It is also wasteful and inefficient of that locality's cultural capital. Investment is needed to gain educational returns on such capital for 'the link between economic and cultural capital is established through the mediation of the time needed for acquisition' (Bourdieu 1997). Educators, learners and families need support, practical leadership and resources to enact the local and regional curriculum development which can offer communities equitable access to their own educational and cultural capital.

Such curricular autonomy would aim to reinforce and reflect the pursuit of 'critical reason' (Beck 1996 p. 194) for learners and teachers. It might attempt to 'liberate people's minds from the limited horizons of whatever more localised cultures they are born into' (ibid.). Equally it would not undermine or ignore such a culture, looking impatiently and transparently through the local to privilege the national or global. Perhaps the cleverest educational response to cultural diversity and systemic globalisation is to build from the local outwards; to offer communities access to the best and most diverse of the national through the curriculum, whilst encouraging a confident autonomy. This could in Beck's words result in 'less need to agonise over how many examples of plays by

Shakespeare . . . should be required reading for 'British' children' (1996 p. 195). Such a clearer sense of what is local, English, European and global about our history cannot coexist with present preoccupations to tell the whole of the 'British' story of history, via the confusions of a 'national' curriculum.

Past and Future Literacy?

In the context of a recent discussion about relationships between gender and achievements in literacy, itself prompted by a consensual concern over boys' perceivedly poor school literacy as compared to girls, Barrs (1998) commented on the importance of enticement in educational texts. Following a well-trodden constructivist route, she argued that readers bring their own identity to text as a way of 'seeking themselves'; and that if insufficient of themselves is reflected in the text it may be discarded. Readers also seek difference, to 'extend ourselves through reading . . . to explore lives which are different from our own' (Barrs 1998 p. 3). Learning history offers just such a textual balance, between building on the familiar and exploring the strange: though this only happens if teachers flesh the skeletal national curriculum with the muscle of real historical sources and texts. Learning history fits in this respect neatly with literacy strategies emphasising textual variety. It also extends them. For learning history is not just about decoding semantic texts. It involves the learner in decoding big ideas about cultures from small fragments of evidence, evidence which may be visual, aural or built, as much as linguistic. Often, though not always, the cultures studied can trace a direct lineage to the ones in which learners live. Becoming literate through history therefore involves reading words, sentences and texts but extends into reading artefacts, arts, cultures and self. This sounds grandiose but in practice need not be. For instance it can start with asking children to write about history learning by including 'magic words' like 'because, during, after, so that'. In an American context Barton and Levstik describe around fifty such 'subordinating conjunctions and prepositions', known in most children's speech but rarely in writing. 'These words call attention to the relationships that lie at the heart of history – how one things causes another, what events came before or after others, and so on . . .' (1997 p. 165). Becoming literate in a *semantic* sense involves the phonetic mastery of relatively simple words, such as these written by an American schoolchild: 'Because Francis Drake stole money and land, he was a hero to England' (ibid.). Becoming literate in a *cultural* sense involves thinking about why Drake became an English hero; or whether theft and heroism are compatible; or whether Drake should still be considered 'heroic'. If history as a discipline is to survive in schools, it must contribute to both.

If it is to prosper in families and communities history education should also remember that people of any age can improve their literacy through learning about history. This practitioner and researcher describes offering a group of female adult literacy learners sociological material from the 1930s and 1940s, plus historical autobiography, fiction and poetry. These acted as a stimulus to their own talking and writing about memories and experiences of motherhood.

> I had wanted to suggest that history has many sources . . . It was as if a tap had been turned on. The talk flowed . . . discussion leaders were awash with words . . . Many of the women . . . spoke of a new enthusiasm for history, hitherto seen as a dry affair.
>
> (Mace 1998 pp. 140–1)

Their talk, writing and subsequent investigations also helped reveal individual identities behind mother-figures and supported at least some of the group's personal and affective understandings. History here is not just a subject learnt in school, an arena for literacy, or a discipline promoting thinking. It is a step forwards through personal and social learning, towards the humane ambition of wisdom.

Such steps need not happen on paper. Although the 'permeation of computers into the compulsory educational setting has been, at best, limited' (Selwyn 1999 p. 78) the pressure for ICT to be deployed in all teaching and learning, including history, is intense. This requirement from the 2000 national curriculum, for instance, could easily have been written about history:

> Pupils should be given opportunities to support their work by being taught to find things out from a variety of sources, selecting and synthesising the information to meet their needs and developing an ability to question its accuracy, bias and plausibility.
>
> (DfEE 1999c p. 39)

It is actually one of five stipulations for the use of information and communication technology across the curriculum. Such official requirements are not the only spur. Another is that learners generally enjoy becoming fluent with ICT tools, just as they like to be literate. When it works, ICT improves people as well as schools: 'Learning is in the co-ordination between language and experience . . . technology increases the range and nature of experiences that can be provided for the learning of subject matters that are complex and abstract' (Saljo 1999 p. 159). Becoming more literate in words, technologies and cultures entails a process of thinking through them. Thinking through history as the masterpiece, perhaps, constructed with whatever technological tools lie in the apprentice's bag. Up until the end of the eighteenth century theses were talk, story, poetry, song, pictures, sculptures, buildings, pens, paper, books and print. In the nineteenth and twentieth centuries photographs, telegraphs, telephones, film, radio, tapes and television were added, amongst others. Word processing, databases, computer modelling and simulations, email, the worldwide web and other internet applications are becoming ubiquitous in the twenty-first. Throughout, the task of teachers remains the same: critically to mediate culture and skilfully to induct learners into thinking about that culture, through the tools and technologies at hand.

Can History Survive?

Such a question helps answer the previous discussion of literacy and technology. History cannot and will not 'survive' in school curricula if it becomes isolated from what curriculum decision makers and stakeholders believe curricula to be for: 'The curriculum itself cannot remain static . . . Education only flourishes if it successfully adapts to the demands and needs of the time' (DfEE 1999c p. 13). This means history helping children to acquire linguistic, cultural and technological literacies, within and beyond history lessons. It also means history educators demonstrating, whether at school or national level, that this is beneficial and it is happening. Spiritual, moral, social and cultural development; personal, social and health education and citizenship; key skills and thinking skills: these may appear to some specialists as generalised overlays obscuring 'subjects' in the English National Curriculum (DfEE 1999 pp. 10–23, 136–41). To this writer they are, and always have been, central to the educational claims of a discipline such as history.

This book has also argued that teachers play a pivotal practical and ethical role in mediating central curricular visions, in the interests of learners as well as themselves. This is a tall order. It demands that teachers reconcile central, supposedly democratic mandates over a national curriculum whilst having an eye behind it to learners and beyond it to its curricular successors. We have to balance keeping a clear focus on what is educationally distinctive about a discipline such as history, to which the various English national curricula have contributed greatly, with seeing how history learning relates to, is extended or even replaced by learning occurring across the curriculum.

Though this is daunting, the alternative is harsh. The further curricular pressures build from learning theory, utilitarian and individualist thinking, the more future curricula need to balance history as a worthwhile discipline in its own right, whilst showing it relating to others. History needs to become interdisciplinary and in so doing, for the secondary phase in particular, to learn from best practice in primary classrooms:

> History is not a subject that can be taught as an exclusive. To teach history well requires that children are aware of all the areas of their life that history touches, from the origins of the the mathematics they are working on, to their right to a free education . . . to teach history in isolation would be a horrible waste of a universal discipline.
>
> (Davies and Redmond 1998 p. 39)

Not just learning through history about locality, literacy or technology for instance: but about how 'the arts' in history lessons can help solve problems and encourage risk taking and creativity (DfEE 1999d). As this American teacher claimed whilst discussing learning history through visual or dramatic art 'It's more fun for me as a teacher and I think that it makes it more interesting for the students. With the arts . . . you take what you learn into your being' (Levstik and Barton 1997 p. 158). In this vision history's curricular worth resides not in the paper, but the person: a living proof of how history can prosper. Now there is a curricular dream worth fighting for . . .

Citizens of History?

If history in England is to make a telling contribution towards citizenship education, it would do well to heed experiences in countries with citizens, not subjects. This brief section therefore looks to America, for instance, from where these historiographers and educators speak:

> History is a disciplined inquiry about past events, separate from what the guardians of nationalism might want its citizens to believe . . .. A democratic nation . . . embraces a citizenry much fuller than its official representation . . . National leaders try to control the collective memory in order to forge a civic identity, while other groups . . . recount particular stories to build solidarity, often in defiance of those seeking a shared past.
>
> (Appleby, Hunt and Jacob 1994 p. 155)

One important contribution of history to citizenship is therefore to record competing stories of identity. This is something which the sub-plots of the current English national curriculum, embodying as they do disputes about intepretations and evidence, achieve much better than their chapter headings, entitled mostly by outmoded claims to a contested 'British' nationalism. Another contribution is to remind educators, as this American does, that students have a right to 'willed not-learning . . . a conscious and chosen refusal to assent to learn' (Kohl 1994 p. 27). 'Not-learning' may sound unreasonable, if it is accepted that school curricula are reasonable: what if, from the perspective of learners, they are not? What if children have never understood why they are being taught history, through years of subjection to it? Would it be reasonable for them to continue trying to learn it? What if children learning about history only ever learned what adults did in history, and not people of their age? What if children from one ethnic minority only ever heard about what a very different ethnic majority did in 'its' history? What if children who lived in England studied a history curriculum which was so muddled about Englishness that it covered its own confusion, by calling it British? Would willed 'not-learning' be a reasonable response to these conditions and might such conditions prevail in many English schools?

It is not only America which can ask England useful questions about education, citizenship and history. Research in England and Malta at the end of the 1990s revealed interesting contrasts in history teachers' attitudes towards the teaching of national history. English teachers construed a 'nationalistic approach' in history teaching almost entirely negatively, their responses being categorised under promoting egocentricity, exultation of own achievements, prejudice, narrowness, manipulation and superiority. Maltese teachers answered the same question with positive or more neutral constructions. These associated a nationalistic approach with making national history predominantly important, fostering love and respect for national identity, with comparisons, interpretations or merely traditional teaching (Vella 1999 p. 14). Although the research needs extending if its analyses are to be reliable, it reveals underlying questions facing history's contribution to English citizenship education. If nationalism is associated in

English teaching minds with negative attributes, how can English national history or identity be discussed in as balanced a way as, say, most teachers would hope to adopt towards French, American or Indian history? And how can history teachers tolerate teaching a history curriculum predicated upon nation-state stories, as is much of the English national history curriculum for ages seven to fourteen?

Beyond History Curricula?

History was invented before schools in their current form existed and has been evident in societies without schools (see Bage 1999a; Samuel 1994). So much so that it is difficult to find an example of, or even imagine a society, in which learning from past experience was not a central feature of education and culture. It could even be claimed that since education connects past knowledge with present and future knowledge, leading the process of helping individuals learn from society, it is inevitably social and historical. Images and stories in different media teach people about history through 'books, newspapers and periodicals ... wireless, cinema and stage'. That was a view from half a century ago (Ministry of Education 1952 p. 81) before mass televisual or internet consumption: how much truer is it now? Children learn history from society, as well as schools.

From a child's perspective the history 'curriculum' may also be of more distant significance to their learning than first readings would suggest. Children experience teachers and teachers' interpretation of curricula in lessons; they do not experience curricula themselves, in a disembodied way. Their learning of history is led by what individual teachers know and how individual teachers behave in history: it is individual and social learning, as much as it is theoretical and intellectual. So, how and what do teachers think about history?

Some research in three English primary schools (Huggins 1996) suggested that experienced teachers' understandings of why they teach history are tacit, at best. Wider ranging research in which the author was involved (Bage, Grisdale and Lister 1999) asked a slightly different question: could teachers articulate gains they had seen their children make through history? Twenty of the twenty-eight teachers could, though the examples cited reflected only a few of the general justifications for history claimed in early national curriculum documents (e.g. DES 1990): comparisons of past and present by children, learning about the past as an end in itself and developing senses of identity featured. Yet when asked a similar question about particular parts of history, namely what children gained from learning about the Ancient Greeks and Romans in Britain, even the few history-specific attributes mentioned above disappeared. Instead, teachers waxed lyrical about how such studies developed study skills, linguistic ability or enhanced pupil motivation (Bage, Grisdale and Lister 1999 pp. 7–9). For these primary teachers of history, of whom a third were the subject's coordinators, history at such close quarters seemed an inter-disciplinary activity or vehicle, as much a specific discipline. Teaching and justifying history at the level of practice, at least in primary schools, bears some but not a clear or immediate relationship to what is happening at the level of subject specialisation. Children's understandings of why they learnt history echoed such findings.

This is not to argue that children did not enjoy or benefit from learning history. Encouragingly, when asked baldly to explain 'what history was' 106 out of 120 children could offer an unprompted definition, in their own words. Fifty-four children's responses led by referring explicity to particular parts of history and another thirty-five led by referring to learning about history. In other words two thirds of a sample of 120 English children aged 7 to 12, of varied attainment in history and from a wide social and geographical spread, could explain what learning history was about for them, in recognisable and overwhelmingly positive terms. What hardly any of them did, as indeed was the case with their teachers, was to reflect back what history curriculum designers had claimed as the best general reasons for learning history, or national curriculum history's particular objectives. For better or worse, political and public rhetoric about history curricula does not seem to bear an easy or straightforward relationship with how teaching and learning are experienced at grassroots level. Whether derived from unthinking conservatism, wilful resistance or lack of investment it seems that what is learnt and taught in history not only should remain at arm's length from what is legislated for in curricula, but will do so regardless. History learning has a mind of its own: long may it live so.

Past into Future?

As an alert reader you will have spotted long before this conclusion exactly how this argument is being built. The last issue I have chosen to highlight, the social issue, will claim that the past can enrich the future by paying heed to the arguments that preceded it. Not just out there in our schools and communities, but also here in this chapter. Thus more local control of curricula; a recognition of history's place in teaching all sorts of literacies; a valuing of history as an inter-disciplinary activity; a commitment to critical, diverse but confident under-standings of identity and nationality; and an acknowledgement of a degree of learners' and teachers' independence from curricula. All these things, I am claiming, will help history contribute to our educational future, and help you as reader to make sense of this book.

This is partly because teaching, as a formal act, is most often intergener-ational. Concluding his exploration of pedagogy this North American educator made a personal observation with which many readers will empathise. It also illustrates the point that teaching and parenting are activities centrally and often uncomfortably concerned with mediating past through present into future:

> As I consider my ten year old son's request to see a particular movie, I cannot forget the things my parents and their generation found appropriate for me when I was a ten year old . . . At the same time I cannot help notice that my child already lives in a world of the future – a world in which the question of what is good for a child is less clearly anchored than the way my parents viewed it, or from the way it was viewed by my parents' parents.
>
> (Van Manen 1991 p. 214)

Where worlds change fast it seems sensible for schools and their curricula to teach children how to cope with change. Instead, many people who have been to school discover they only learn this for themselves, after leaving. Some even make a living out of telling us all about how to exist 'beyond certainty':

> When I went to school, I did not learn anything much . . . except for this hidden message, that every major problem in life had already been solved . . . That hidden message from my school, I eventually realized, was not only crippling, it was wrong . . .

> (Handy 1996 pp. 16–17)

Can education shift 'beyond certainty'? Can we learn to extend the present by constructing it in different ways? Educators may need to think deeply about time, change and continuity to achieve this. Even if successful we are only playing tag with science: 'Plutonium is a lethal, man-made substance with a half-life of about 250,000 years. In this respect our culture is already in the future' (Beare and Slaughter 1993 p. 116). If unsuccessful . . . what will come to pass? Conventional school history seems to have little to offer on this. As an eminent English educator and historian commented 'there is no evidence that school pupils translate their knowledge of the past into an understanding of the present unless the past is explicitly related to current circumstances' (Slater 1995 p. 146).

What of unconventional school history? From a European perspective another critic has intriguingly suggested that a history of the future should be included in the curriculum. He described how predictions are served up to modern cultures through the mass media by futurologists and science fiction, as well as by politicians and astrologers, and argued that 'no history should end at the present day but must go on to critically examine the different ways in which the future is currently represented' (Cajani 1992 p. 63).

When I first read this, I thought it was barmy. When I second read it, I chortled. By the third reading I was convinced of its brilliance. What could be more obvious? Rather than ending history awkwardly in the present or recent past, we extend it into examining visions of the future. On these we focus all that we have learnt from history: skills and knowledge, values and attitudes, both personal and public. Then we use what we learn not to pretend that past, present and future are simplistically the same; but to examine how they are linked, how they differ and how we struggle to make sense from them all.

Which is just what I hope you will have done with this book . . .

References

ACCAC (1999) *History in the Welsh Curriculum – Draft Proposals*, Cardiff: The Qualifications, Curriculum and Assessment Authority for Wales.

Ainscow, M., Hopkins, D., Southworth, G. and West, M. (1994) *Creating the Conditions for School Improvement: a handbook of staff development activities*, London: David Fulton.

Aldrich, R. (1988) 'Imperialism in the study and teaching of history' in Mangan, J. (ed.) *Benefits Bestowed? Education and British Imperialism*, Manchester: Manchester University Press.

Alexander, P., Schallert, D. and Hare, V. (1991) 'Coming to terms: how researchers in learning and literacy talk about knowledge', *Review of Educational Research,* **61** (3) pp. 315–43.

Alexander, R. (1984) *Primary Teaching*, London: Holt, Rinehart and Winston.

Alexander, R. (1995) *Versions of Primary Education*, London: Routledge.

Alexander, R. (ed.) (1997) *Time for Change? Primary curriculum managers at work*, Warwick: Centre for Research in Elementary and Primary Education.

Alexander, R. (1998) 'Basics, cores and choices: towards a new primary curriculum', *Education 3–13* pp. 60–9.

Anderson, D. (1997) *A Common Wealth – Museums and Learning in the United Kingdom*, London: Department of National Heritage.

Applebee, A. (1978) *The Child's Concept of Story*, Chicago/London: Chicago University Press.

Appleby, J., Hunt, L. and Jacob, M. (1994) *Telling the Truth about History*, New York: W. W. Norton & Co.

Ashe, G. (1990) *Mythology of the British Isles*, London: Methuen.

Askew, S. and Carnell, E. (1998) *Transforming Learning: Individual and Global Change*, London: Cassell.

Aves, P. (1998) *Life, Death and Ancient Egypt: aspects of teaching history with reference to the Nuffield History Project 1996–98*, unpublished assignment, submitted for a Certificate in Further Professional Studies, Cambridge University School of Education.

Bage, G. (1993) 'History at KS1 and KS2', *Curriculum Journal* **4** (2) Summer 1993 pp. 269–82.

Bage, G. (1997) 'The magic of monitoring', *Managing Schools Today* **6** (6) pp. 26–8.

Bage, G. (1998) 'Today's history: primary sources', *History Today* **48** (12) pp. 14–15.

Bage, G. (1999a) *Narrative Matters: teaching and learning history through story*, London: Falmer Press.

Bage, G. (1999b) with Grosvenor, J. and Williams, M. 'Curriculum planning: prediction or response? A case study of teacher planning conducted through Partnership Action Research', *Curriculum Journal* **10** (1) pp. 49–69.

Bage, G. (2000a) 'Developing teaching as storytelling' in Cliff Hodges, G., Drummond, M. Styles, M. (eds) *Tales, Tellers and Texts*, London: Cassell.

Bage, G. (2000b) 'Tales for millennial teaching?', *Education 3–13*, Special Edition.

Bage, G., Grisdale R. and Lister, R. (1999) *Classical History in Primary Schools: teaching and learning at Key Stage 2*, London: QCA.

Ball, S. (1994) *Education Reform: a critical and post-structuralist perspective*, Buckingham: OUP.

Barnes, D. (1976) *From Communication to Curriculum*, London: Penguin.

Barnes, J. (1989) *The History of the World in Ten and a Half Chapters*, Cambridge: Cambridge University Press (1995) edition.

Barnes, J. (1998) *England, England*, London: Picador (1999) edition.

Barrs, M. (1998) 'Texts and Subtexts' in Barrs, M. and Pidgeon, S. (eds) *Boys and Reading*, London: Centre for Language in Primary Education.

Bassey, M. (1995) *Creating Education Through Research*, Newark: Kirklington Moor Press.

Beare, H. and Slaughter, R. (1993) *Education for the Twenty-First Century*, London: Routledge.

Beck, J. (1996) 'Nation, curriculum and identity in conservative cultural analysis: a critical commentary', *Cambridge Journal of Education*, **26** (2) pp. 171–98.

Berlak, A. and Berlak, H. (1981) *Dilemmas of Schooling: teaching and social change*, London: Methuen.

Blyth, A. (1994) 'History and Geography in the Primary curriculum' in Bourne, J. (ed.) *Thinking Through Primary Practice*, London: Routledge.

Bourdieu, P. (1997, first published 1986) 'The Forms of Capital' in Halsey, A., Lauder, H., Brown, P. and Stuart Wells, A. (1997) *Education: Culture, Economy, Society*, Oxford: Oxford University Press.

Bridge, G. (1907) 'History: what to teach and what not to teach', *The Journal of Education* May 1907 pp. 323–6.

Brookfield, S. (1995) *Becoming a Critically Reflective Teacher*, San Francisco, CA: Jossey-Bass.

Brooks, R., Aris, M. and Perry, I. (1993) *The Effective Teaching of History*, London: Longman.

Brown, R. (1995) *Managing the Learning of History*, London: David Fulton.

Bruner, J. (1983) *In Search of Mind: essays in autobiography*, New York: Harper and Row.

Bruner, J. (1986) *Actual Minds, Possible Worlds*, London: Harvard University Press.

Bruner, J. (1996) *The Culture of Education*, London: Harvard University Press.

Cajani, L. (1992) 'Past and Future, or History Textbooks and the Obscure Object of Desire' in Bourdillon, H. (ed.) *History and Social Studies – Methodologies of Textbook Analysis*, published for the Council of Europe, Amsterdam: Swets & Zeitlinger.

Callcott (Lady) (1878) *Little Arthur's England*, London: John Murray.

Chancellor, V. (1970) *History for their Masters: opinion in the English history textbook, 1800–1914*, Bath: Adams and Dart.

Chong, J. (1997) *Rhetoric and Reality: a study of whether a pyschologically based theory, Multiple Intelligences [Gardner 1984] can be effectively used to plan and teach a history National Curriculum unit*, unpublished M.Ed Thesis, Cambridge University School of Education.

Claire, H. (1996) *Reclaiming Our Pasts – equality and diversity in the primary history curriculum*, Stoke: Trentham Books.

References

Cole, M. (1998) 'Racism, reconstructed multiculturalism and antiracist education', *Cambridge Journal of Education*, **28** (1) pp. 37–48.

Colley, L. (1992) *Britons: Forging the Nation 1707–1837*, London: Yale University Press.

Collicott, S. (1986) *Connections: Haringey local-national-world links*, London: Haringey Community Information Service, for the Multi-Cultural Curriculum Support Group.

Collicott, S. (1990) 'Who is the national history curriculum for?', *Teaching History*, **61** October 1990 pp. 8–12.

Collicott, S. (1992) 'Who is forgotten in HSU Britain since the 1930s?', *Primary Teaching Studies*, **6** (3) pp. 252–68.

Collicott, S. (1993) 'A way of looking at history: local-national-world links', *Teaching History*, July pp. 18–23.

Collins, F. (1999) 'Bringing history alive' in *Language Matters*, Spring 1999, journal of Centre for Language in Primary Education.

Collins, F. (2000a) 'Storyseeds: Creating Curriculum Stories' in Cliff Hodges, G., Drummond, M., Styles, M. (eds) *Tales, Tellers and Texts*, London: Cassell.

Collins, F. and Hollinshead, L. (2000b) *English and the Historic Environment: a teacher's guide*, London: English Heritage.

Conle, C. (1997) 'Images of change in narrative', *Teachers and Teaching: theory and practice*, **3** (2) pp. 205–19.

Cooper, H. (1995a) *History in the Early Years*, London: Routledge.

Cooper, H. (1995b) *The Teaching of History. Implementing the Revised National Curriculum*, London: David Fulton.

Cooper, H. (1998) 'English across the curriculum: History in its own write 2', *Primary English Magazine*, January/February 1998 pp. 16–18.

Cooper, P. and McIntyre, D. (1996) *Effective Teaching and Learning: teachers' and students' perspectives*, Buckingham: Open University Press.

Counsell, C. (1997) *Analytical and Discursive Writing at Key Stage 3*, London: Historical Association.

Crawford, K. (1995) 'A history of the Right: the battle for control of national curriculum history', *British Journal of Educational Studies*, **43**, 4, pp. 433–56.

Crites, S. (1986) 'Story time: Recollecting the Past and Projecting the Future' in Sarbin, T.(ed.), *Narrative Psychology*, New York: Praeger.

Cullingford, C. (1995) *The Effective Teacher*, London: Cassell.

Dadds, M. (1998) 'Some Politics of Pedagogy', paper delivered to the Standing Conference for the Education and Training of Teachers (1998).

Daily Mail (1992) 'This history is bunk', 15 October.

Davies, J. and Redmond, J. (1998) *Coordinating History Across the Primary School*, London: Falmer Press.

Day, C. (1999) *Developing Teachers: the challenges of lifelong learning*, London: Falmer Press.

DES (1989) *Aspects of Primary Education: the teaching and learning of History and Geography*, London: HMSO.

DES (1990 April) *National Curriculum History Working Group*, London: HMSO.

DES (1991) *History in the National Curriculum – Final Order*, London: HMSO.

DES (1995) *History in the National Curriculum*, London: HMSO.

DfEE (1997) *Excellence in Schools*, London: DfEE.

DfEE (1998) *The National Literacy Strategy – framework for teaching*, London: DfEE.

DfEE (1999a) *History: the national curriculum for England key stages 1–3*, London: DfEE.

DfEE (1999b) *The National Curriculum Handbook for Primary Teachers in England*, London: DfEE.

DfEE (1999c) *The National Curriculum Handbook for Secondary Teachers in England*, London: DfEE.

DfEE (1999d) *All Our Futures: creativity, culture and education*, report of the National Advisory Committee on Creative and Cultural Education, London: DfEE.

Dingsdale, A. (1998) *Ignatius Sancho (1729–1780) Life and Times*, London: Greenwich Education Services.

Dittmer, A. and Fischetti, J. (1995) 'Foxfire and Teacher Preparation: Practising what we Teach' in Wideen, M. and Grimmett, P. (eds) *Changing Times in Teacher Education: restructuring or reconceptualisation?*, London: Falmer Press.

Donaldson, M. (1978) *Children's Minds*, London: Fontana.

Dow, P. (1991) *Schoolhouse Politics: lessons from the Sputnik era*, London: Harvard University Press.

Edwards, A. (1978) 'The Language of History and the Communication of Historical Knowledge' in Dickinson, A. and Lee, P. *History Teaching and Historical Understanding*, London: Heinemann.

Eisner, E. (1994) *Cognition and Curriculum Reconsidered*, London: Teachers College Press.

Elbaz, F. (1991) 'Research on teacher's knowledge', *Journal of Curriculum Studies*, **23** (1) pp. 1–19.

Farmer, A. and Knight, P. (1995) *Active History in Key Stages 3 and 4*, London: David Fulton.

Findlay, J.(ed.) (n.d.) *The School and the Child: being selections from the educational essays of John Dewey*, London: Blackie & Son.

Fines, J. and Nichol, J. (1997) *Teaching Primary History*, London: Heinemann.

Fisher, P. (1999) 'Analysing Anne Frank: a case study in the teaching of thinking skills' *Teaching History*, **95** pp. 24–31.

Fletcher, S. (1907) 'Idola Pulpitorum: the pitfalls of the practical teacher', *The Journal of Education*, June pp. 381–3.

Fletcher, C. and Kipling, R. (1911) *A School History of England*, London: Hodder and Stoughton.

Froggatt, N. (1998) *The Story of How I Became a Teacher of History*, unpublished Cambridgeshire Nuffield History Project Assignment, University of Cambridge School of Education.

Galton, M.(1995) *Crisis in the Primary Classroom*, London: David Fulton.

Gardner, H. (1993) *The Unschooled Mind: how children think and how schools should teach*, London: Fontana Press.

Gardner, P. (1993) 'Uncertainty, teaching and personal autonomy', *Cambridge Journal of Education*, **23** (2) pp. 155–71.

Garrison, L. (1994) 'The Black Historical Past in British Education' in Stone, P. and Mackenzie, R. (eds) *The Excluded Past: archaeology in education*, London: Routledge.

Gillborn, D. (1997) 'Racism and reform: new ethnicities/old inequalities?', *British Educational Research Journal* **23** (3) pp. 345–60.

Gosden, P. (1969) *How They Were Taught: an anthology of contemporary accounts of learning and teaching in England 1800–1950*, Oxford: Basil Blackwell.

Griffiths, M. (1995) 'Autobiography, Feminism and the Practice of Action Research' in Thomas, D. *Teachers' Stories*, Buckingham: Open University Press.

Grosvenor, I. (1999) 'History and the perils of multiculturalism in 1990s Britain', *Teaching History*, **97** pp. 37–40.

References

The Guardian (1999) 'Tories protest at history shift', 5 August.

HA (1999) 'Draft National Curriculum Orders: History. A response by the Historical Association', unpublished policy document, Historical Association, 59a Kennington Park Road, London SE11 4JH.

Hadyn, T., Arthur J. and Hunt, M. (1997) *Learning to Teach History in the Secondary School: a companion to school experience*, London: Routledge.

Hamer, J. (1997) 'History in the Primary Years: the state of the nation', *Primary History* 17 November pp. 14–15.

Handy, C. (1996) *Beyond Certainty*, London: Arrow Books.

Hargreaves, A. (1994) *Changing Teachers, Changing Times: teachers' work and culture in the postmodern age*, London: Cassell.

Hazareesingh, S. (1994) *Speaking About The Past. Oral History for 5–7 Year Olds*, Stoke: Trentham Books.

HCP (1970) *The Humanities Curriculum Project an Introduction*, London: Heinemann.

Hewitt, R. (1996) *Routes of Racism: the social basis of racist action*, Trentham Books: Stoke.

Hoodless, P. (1996) 'Children Talking About the Past' in Hall, N. and Martello, J. (eds) *Listening to Children Think: exploring talk in the early years*, London: Hodder and Stoughton.

Hoodless, P. (ed.) (1998) *History and English in the Primary School*, London: Routledge.

Howard, M. (1905) 'A plea for a history room in schools', *The Journal of Education*, May 1905 pp. 367–8.

Hoyle, E. and John, P. (1995) *Professional Knowledge and Professional Practice*, London: Cassell.

Huggins, M. (1996) 'An analysis of the rationales for learning history given by children and teachers at Key Stage 2', *The Curriculum Journal*, **7** (3) pp. 307–21.

Hull, R. (1986) *The Language Gap*, London: Methuen.

Humphries, S. (1981) *Hooligans or Rebels?*, Oxford: Blackwell.

Husbands, C. (1996) *What Is History Teaching? Language, ideas and meaning in learning about the past*, Buckingham: OUP.

Hutton, P. (1993) *History as an Art of Memory*, Hanover: University Press of New England.

Joseph, Sir K. (1984) 'Why Teach History in School?' Speech to the Historical Association conference 10 February 1984, published in *The Historian* (2).

Kohl, H. (1994) *I Won't Learn From You and Other Thoughts on Creative Maladjustment*, New York: New Press.

Kolb, D. (1976) *Learning Style Inventory: Technical Manual*, Boston: McBer and Co.

Lee, P. (1984) 'Historical Imagination' in Dickinson, A. (ed.) *Learning History*, London: Heinemann.

Lee, P. (1991) 'Historical Knowledge and the National Curriculum' in Aldrich, R. (ed.) *History in the National Curriculum*, London: Kogan Page.

Lee, P., Ashby, R. and Dickinson, A. (1996) 'Progression in children's ideas about history' in Hughes, M. *Progression in Learning*, Clevedon: Multilingual Matters.

Leinster-Mackay, D. (1988) 'The Nineteenth-century English Preparatory School: Cradle and Creche of Empire?' in Mangan, J. (ed.) *Benefits Bestowed? Education and British Imperialism*, Manchester: Manchester University Press.

Levstik, L. and Barton, K. (1997) *Doing History: investigating with children in Elementary and Middle Schools*, New Jersey: Lawrence Erlbaum Associates.

Lively, P. (1987) *Moon Tiger*, London: Penguin.

Lomas, T. (1999) 'The Historical Association's response to the Curriculum 2000 proposals', *Primary History*, **23** p. 6.

Lowenthal, D. (1998) *The Heritage Crusade and the Spoils of History*, Cambridge: Cambridge University Press.

MacDonald, F. and Starkey, D. (1996) *Read Aloud History Stories*, London: Harper Collins.

Mace, J. (1998) *Playing with Time: mothers and the meaning of literacy*, London: UCL Press.

MacIntyre, A. (1981) *After Virtue*, London: Duckworth Press.

McKiernan, D. (1993) 'Imagining the nation at the end of the 20th century', *Journal of Curriculum Studies*, **25** (1) pp. 33–51.

Macpherson, W. (1999) *The Stephen Lawrence Inquiry: report of an inquiry by Sir William Macpherson of Cluny*, London: The Stationery Office.

Mann, J. (1997) *How my understanding of history and learning has developed during the Nuffield History Project*, unpublished Assignment for a Certificate in Further Professional Study, Cambridge University School of Education.

Michaels, A. (1996) *Fugitive Pieces*, London: Bloomsbury Publishing.

Ministry of Education (1952) *Teaching History*, London: HMSO.

Morris, E. (1997) Speech to the *SCAA Curriculum Conference*, 9/10 June 1997.

Morton, J. (1993) 'How young pupils' memories work', *Topic* (10) Autumn 1993 pp. 1–7.

Neild, N. (1907) 'Some criticisms of modern methods of teaching history', *Journal of Education*, April 1907 pp. 290–2.

Nicol, J. with Dean, J. (1997) *History 7–11: developing primary teaching skills*, London: Routledge.

OFSTED (1995) *History: A review of inspection findings 1993/94*, London: HMSO.

OFSTED (1997) *National Curriculum Assessment Results and the Wider Curriculum at Key Stage 2* – some evidence from the OFSTED database (OFSTED and DfEE November 1997).

OXFAM (1999) *Put Yourself On The Line: a teacher's guide to active global citizenship*, Oxford: Oxfam Development Education Programme.

Paine, T. (1992) *Rights of Man Part II*, Collins, H. (ed.), London: Penguin Books (1969 edition).

Pankhania, J. (1994) *Liberating the National History Curriculum*, London: Falmer Press.

Paxton, R. (1997) 'Someone with like a life wrote it: the effects of a visible author on High School history students', *Journal of Educational Psychology*, **89** (2) pp. 235–50.

Phillips, R. (1998) *History Teaching, Nationhood and the State: a study in educational politics*, London: Cassell.

Polan, D. (1996) 'The Professors of History' in Sobchack, V. (ed.) *The Persistence of History: cinema, television and the modern event*, London: Routledge.

Pollard, A., Broadfoot, P., Osborn, M. and Abbott, D. (1994) *Changing English Primary Schools? The Impact of the Educational Reform Act at KS1*, London: Cassell.

QCA (1998) *Developing the School Curriculum: advice to the Secretary of State and his response on the broad nature and scope of the review of the National Curriculum*, London: QCA.

Rashid, N. and Gregory, E. (1997) 'Learning to Read, Reading to Learn: the Importance of Siblings in the Language and Development of Young Bilingual Children', in Gregory, E. (ed.) *One Child, Many Worlds: early learning in multicultural communities*, London: David Fulton.

Reynolds, J. (1996) 'An Ear to the Ground: Learning Through Talking' in Bearne, E. (ed.) *Differentiation and diversity in the primary school*, London: Routledge.

Saljo, R. (1999) 'Learning as the Use of Tools: a Sociocultural Perspective on the Human–Technology Link' in Littleton, K. and Light, P. (eds) *Learning with Computers: analysing productive interaction*, London: Routledge.

References

Samuel, R. (1994) *Theatres of Memory*, London: Verso.

Seixas, P. (1999) 'Beyond content and pedagogy: in search of a way to talk about history education', *Journal of Curriculum Studies*, **31** (3) pp. 317–37.

Selwyn, N. (1999) 'Why the computer is not dominating schools: a failure of policy or a failure of practice?', *Cambridge Journal of Education*, **29** (1) pp. 77–91.

Short, G.and Carrington, B. (1998) 'Reconstructing multicultural education: a response to Mike Cole', *Cambridge Journal of Education*, **28** (2) pp. 231–8.

Shorto, A. (1908) 'The use of local history to the teacher', *The Journal of Education*, July 1908 pp. 499–501.

Simon, J. (1966) *Education and Society in Tudor England*, Cambridge: Cambridge University Press.

Sinclair, I. (1999) *Sorry Meniscus: excursions to the Millennium Dome*, London: Profile Books.

Slater, J. (1995) *Teaching History in the New Europe*, published for the Council of Europe, London: Cassell.

Sobel, D. (1995) *Longitude*, London: Fourth Estate.

Southgate, B. (1996) *History: What & Why? Ancient, modern and postmodern perspectives*, London: Routledge.

Stenhouse, L. (1975) *An Introduction to Curriculum Research and Development*, London: Heinemann.

Stenhouse, L. (1981) 'What counts as research?', *British Journal of Educational Studies*, **39** (2) pp. 103–13.

Suffolk LEA (1991) *Using Historical Sources in the Classroom* (Guidance Booklet 9), Ipswich: Suffolk Humanities Advisory Team.

Suffolk LEA (1995) *Managing History in the Primary School* (Guidance Booklet 46), Ipswich: Suffolk Humanities Advisory Team.

Sunday Times (1994) 'Britain put at history's heart', 1 May.

Taylor, W. (ed.) (1984) *Metaphors of Education*, London: Heinemann.

Times Educational Supplement (1990) 'McGregor fails to ruffle history critics', 3 August.

Times Educational Supplement (1999) 'Ministers revert to literary tradition', 10 September.

Tonkin, E. (1992) *Narrating Our Pasts: the social construction of oral history*, Cambridge: CUP.

Tremain, R. (1989) *Restoration*, London: Hodder and Stoughton (1990 edition).

Turner-Bisset, R. (1999) 'The knowledge bases of the expert teacher', *British Educational Research Journal*, **25** (1) pp. 39–55.

Unstead, R. J. (1956) *Teaching History in the Junior School*, London: A. & C. Black.

Van Manen, M. (1991) *The Tact of Teaching: the meaning of pedagogical thoughtfulness*, Western Ontario: The Althouse Press.

Vansledright, B. (1997) 'And Santayana lives on: students' views on the purposes for studying American history', *Journal of Curriculum Studies*, **29** (5) pp. 529–57.

Vella, Y. (1999) 'Heritage and national identity in Maltese schools', *EuroClio Bulletin*, **12** pp. 13–14.

Walsh, B. (1998) 'Why Gerry likes history now: the power of the word processor', *Teaching History* (93), pp. 6–15.

Watson, F. (1909) *The Beginnings of the Teaching of Modern Subjects in England*, London: Pitman and Sons. Reprinted 1971 by S. R. Publishers: Wakefield, England.

Weiner, G. (1993) 'Shell-shock or Sisterhood: English School History and Feminist Practice', in Arnot, M. (ed.) *Feminisim and Social Justice in Education*, London: Falmer Press.

Wells, G. (1992) 'The Centrality of Talk in Education' in *Thinking Voices – the work of the National Oracy Project* (pp. 283–310) Norman, K. (ed.), London: Hodder and Stoughton.

White, H. (1987) *The Content of the Form*, New York: Johns Hopkins University Press.

White, J. (1997) 'Three Proposals and a Rejection' in Smith R. and Standish P. (eds) *Teaching Right and Wrong: moral education in the balance*, Stoke: Trentham Books.

Wigginton, E. (1989) 'Foxfire grows up', *Harvard Educational Review*, **59**, pp. 24–49.

Wigginton, E. (1998) 'Reaching Across the Generations: the Foxfire Experience' (first published 1988), in Perks, R. and Thomson, A. (eds) *The Oral History Reader*, London: Routledge.

Williams, A. (1997) 'Investigating Literacy in London: Three Generations of Readers in an East End Family' in Gregory, E. (ed.) *One Child, Many Worlds: early learning in multicultural communities*, London: David Fulton.

Wishart, E. (1986) 'Reading and Understanding History Textbooks' in *The Language of School Subjects* Gilham, B. (ed.), London: Heinemann.

Woodhead, C. (1997) *The Annual Report of Her Majesty's Chief Inspector of Schools*, London: OFSTED.

Woods, P. and Jeffrey, B. (1996) *Teachable Moments: the art of teaching in Primary Schools*, Buckingham: OUP.

Wray, D. and Lewis, M. (1997) *Extending Literacy: children reading and writing non-fiction*, London: Routledge.

Wrenn, A. (1999) 'Build it in, don't bolt it on: history's opportunity to support critical citizenship', *Teaching History* (96), pp. 6–12.

Index

accessibility 81, 125; from clear speech 20–1, 88, 92, 127; from readable text 118–19, 126–7; *see also* equality
Alexander, P., Schallert, D. and Hare, V.: on knowledge 88–90
America: California History-Social Science Project (CH-SSP) 40–2; Foxfire project 71–2, 135–8; historians on citizenship 152
artefacts 9, 96; for literacy hour 114, 115–17; *see also* external aids
assessment 81–2; attainment levels 109–12; criteria 87–8, 105–6; formative 87, 107–8, 109–10; from information 107; limitations 106, 107; of literacy 108, 117–18; prompts 128; from questions 107; student achievement statements 108–10; summative 108; tasks 87, 110–12
authorship 23
autonomy 69–70; from curriculum 10, 46–7, 52–3, 127–9, 137, 146–7, 148, 154; from politicians 154; readers 145–6; *see also* individuals

Blyth, A.: on understanding of time 55–6
British curricula: diversification 67
Brooks, R., Aris, M. and Perry, I.: on curriculum diversification 35–7
Brown, R.: quality principles 38
Bruner, J.: on European powers 23; reasoning specifications 17–18
business ethics: as ideal 62–3

California History-Social Science Project (CH-SSP) 40–2
citizenship 47, 66, 81, 120, 132–3; educators from America on 152; teachers from England on 152–3; teachers from Malta on 152; *see also* identity; morality

Claire, H.: on equality 39
classroom pedagogy: vs written communication 44
collaboration: teacher–pupil 17–18, 137
Collicott, Sylvia: on local history initiatives 72–3
community emphasis *see* local history
context-based curriculum 13
core subjects: vs foundation subjects 62
curriculum *see* national curriculum

Day, C.: on developmental learning 40, 41
discrimination *see* equality
diversification 70; in assessment 87–8; British curricula 67; English curriculum 35–7; of intelligences *see* multiskilling; of media aids *see* multimedia; from multiculturalism 53, 71; national curriculum 53, 71; in role play 82–5; of student objectives 1
documents: content 123; formats 121 (reformatting 124); period analysis 123–4; societal analysis 124; student analysis 122; teacher analysis 121–2

empathy 11, 21, 22–3, 25, 31, 55, 71–2; limitations 48; from photographs 103, 104; from unmodified artefacts 9; *see also* identity; imagination
England: 'Britain' as synonym 68, 69, 148–9, 152; curriculum *see* national curriculum; Greenwich as metaphor 3, 74, 75; imperialism 28, 29–30; multiculturalism *see* multiculturalism; nationalism 152–3
equality 25; from local history 73–4; multiculturalism *see* multiculturalism; national curriculum 53, 71; vs privileged classes 26, 39; vs racism 52, 53, 74–5; vs sexism 39, 52; special needs students 118–19; *see also* accessibility